Solunar Returns

by ANNE. N. VICK

RIGHTLEFT GRAPHICS, CHINO VALLEY, ARIZONA, USA

Vick, Anne N., 1924-2008
        Solunar Returns.
Astrology—Solunar returns
133'5
ISBN: 978-0-9636841-1-0

The cover art is based on what is commonly referred to as the "Flammarion woodcut." The name of the original artist is unknown, however since it first appeared in Camille Flammarion's 1888 book *L'atmosphere: meteorologie populaire*, the woodcut is widely attributed to Flammarion.

Design and layout by Miller *&* Mattson www.millermattson.com

RightLeft Graphics
P.O. Box 153
Chino Valley, Arizona 86323 USA
www.rightleftgraphics.com

This book is dedicated to the memory of Anne Vick, and to her husband Theodore (Ted) F. Vick who was her life partner.

Table of Contents

Forward

As students of astrology you are more than likely intrigued by the multitude of astrological techniques that await you within this ancient craft. This book contains a technique that will not only capture your interest but will likely remain a favorite in your astrology toolbox. The technique called solunar returns was expertly practiced by one of our astrological community's most gifted astrologers, Anne N. Vick. Anne was well known and loved by her community and was best known to the Astrological Society of Arizona. She brought her subject many times to the group and presented her final workshop on Aug 19, 2005. We are very grateful for the devotion of her dear friends at RightLeft Graphics who published her final talk into this powerful book.

You may have peeked at the chart of the Moon's transit to your natal Sun as a simple notion. Intuitively you suspected that such a chart must hold a valuable message. Anne shows us how these monthly charts not only depict a theme for the month, but are actually activated daily and can be viewed as a sort of personal calendar. Anne leaves us her expert treatment of solunars, which goes beyond the initial delineation. She uses the transiting Moon through the houses of the return chart and integrates her other favorite techniques to get the most out of this powerful chart.

From the moment I met Anne Vick in 2003 I knew I was going to have an astrological exchange like no other. I seemed to have serendipitously attracted a seasoned astrologer whom I can only describe as astro-royalty. She articulated her cutting edge methods with the ease of an ancient sage and she shared her knowledge generously, as she did her time and warm heart. Anne's sister-like style instantly brought you inside. If you were interested in astrology, she made your experience worthwhile and enriched your thirst for further study. She was a born teacher of astrology - her lifelong passion.

We met in Newton, Massachusetts while she and her beloved husband Ted visited her daughter's family. She called me after hearing my weekly Saturday radio report to order a copy of my book, Lunar Shadows. We had such a warm exchange we decided to make a long visit which led to a longer visit at her home in Mesa, Arizona. The Arizona Society of Astrologers invited me to speak on my Moon Family topic from my book in 2004. I returned a few years later and found Anne, still forever young at heart and mind, adding an optimistic viewpoint to each challenge she had encountered.

Her astrological knowledge and integration of technique went beyond the comprehension of the average astrologer, however Anne lived in an area where many brilliant astrological minds eagerly exchanged their unique applications in astrology. In her generosity, Anne set aside working on her own book to help edit the still unpublished book of her friend and colleague Virginia Reyer (b. June17, 1925, d. Nov 25, 2008). She also worked with Bonnie Wilson (b. April 28, 1931, d. March 8, 2007), a brilliant horary astrologer whose work is truly missed.

Anne not only favored and perfected her technique of solunars. She would converse freely on a multitude of techniques she had studied and applied and would dovetail nicely into her chart delineations. Anne Vick's solunar insights are a treasure for any serious student of astrology. This is a must-have book.

Stunningly, Anne seemed to have called out to make her most poignant case for the value of solunars when she passed away within hours of her final solunar on December 12, 2008 (you can see the charts in a chapter near the end of this book).

We miss you Anne.

Dietrech Pessin
Newton, Massachusetts
December 2009

Introduction

The Sun is the spirit and giver of life. Your natal sun represents your life purpose, your will, and your drive. The Moon reflects the spirit of the Sun within. Your natal Moon represents your inner self, your sensitivity, and your ability to be flexible. The Sun and its aspects express their energies physically, mentally, and emotionally, while the Moon is expressed emotionally. These energies can be used positively or negatively. This is your free will.

Each day at sunrise, starting at the Eastern horizon, the Sun begins its daily cycle thru the zodiac. The moon takes 28 or 29 days to circle the earth, taking about two and a half days to transit through each sign. Each month, and rarely twice in a month, we have a new Moon or a full Moon which shows us the nature and temperament of that month. The solunar chart is based on the transiting Moon returning to the exact degree of the natal Sun, which happens every month.

The solunar Moon is a new beginning and shows what is ahead for the month, activating the natal chart. The energies of the solunar chart last for only one month, so events will move quickly. This chart is called a personal lunation or a Solunar Return.

About the author

Anne Natalie (Cerrato) Vick was born in 1924 in New Jersey. She was always interested in the zodiac (as it was called then) and laughingly said she had been a gypsy in a previous life, claiming one of her aspirations was to be a hobo. With her restless Gemini spirit, she set herself to all manner of pursuits until, in 1976, she began to study astrology and discovered the passion of her intellectual life.

She was renowned as a counselor, enjoying a loyal clientele from nearly every age-group, walk of life, and continent. She was a dedicated teacher and a much sought-after speaker. Additionally, she was a respected member of astrological societies in both New Jersey and Arizona.

Anne passed from this life in December 2008, and this book represents her latest work on solunar returns. It is based chiefly on a presentation she made to the Arizona Society of Astrologers (ASA) on August 19, 2005 in Phoenix, Arizona, USA. Her husband Ted asked Anne's friend and colleague, Nelda Louise Tanner, to see to its publication.

Anne, with her bountiful insights, knowledge, and wisdom, is missed.

Introduction to solunar returns

What are solunar returns?

When planets return to their natal positions, these are called *planetary returns*. Each year when the transiting Sun returns to its natal position, it is called a *solar return*. Each month when the transiting Moon returns to the natal Sun it is known as a *solunar return*, or often referred to as your *personal new Moon*.

A chart showing your solunar can be used as a daily record and highlights the areas of interest for the month allowing you to plan ahead. Running your solunar return charts several months in advance gives one the opportunity to view the large picture and make necessary adjustments before life comes at you without any warnings.

How solunars came into my life

There are many methods used in forecasting such as progressions, solar arc directions, eclipses, age arc projections, and of course solunar returns.

I was first introduced to solunar returns in the early 1980s. There was very little written about them at that time so I kept searching for any books, tapes, lectures, and workshops I could find to learn more. One day a book list appeared on my desk, and lo and behold there was a book called *The Tropical Solunar Return* by Therese. I quickly sent for it—but it was the wrong topic. I set it aside.

Some time later I saw *Tropical Solunar Return* by T. Rossignal on a list of tapes. I sent for it, but again it was the wrong topic. Now I decided the Universe was trying to send me a message and so I read the book and listened to the tape and discovered they were created by the very same person. This set me off on my own quest to learn about solunars for myself, and I have found it to be an exciting and valuable tool for forecasting each month.

Throughout this work I've used the Koch house system. The charts in this book were run with geocentric, tropical, and true node. Sometimes I rounded the degrees. Some of the Arabian Parts that are used in the examples are as follows:

- Part of Assassination = Ascendant + Ruler of 12th - Neptune
- Part of Catastrophe = Ascendant + Neptune - Saturn
- Part of Divorce = is always opposite Venus
- Part of Death = Ascendant + 8th Cusp - Moon
- Part of Fortune = Ascendant + Moon - Sun
- Part of Marriage = Ascendant + 7th Cusp - Venus
- Part of Suicide = Ascendant + 8th - Neptune
- Part of Surgery = Ascendant + Saturn – Mars

Some of the Midpoints used in the examples are as follows:

- Saturn / Pluto = Mass Murder, Violent people
- Mars / Uranus = Violence, Revolutionaries
- Mars / Saturn = Destructive Energy, Harshness, Bitterness
- Jupiter / Saturn = Patience, Discontent
- Mars / Pluto = Disaster, Catastrophe

I wish to recommend a book called *Personal Lunation Charts* by Helen Paul-Wolf from which I have learned a considerable amount about solunar Charts. It was published in 1988 by the American Federation of Astrologers.

I hope this book will stimulate your interest and curiosity so that you'll add it to your own astrological toolbox and use it as I have.

Setting up the solunar chart

Your solunar, or solunar Moon, is when the transiting moon conjuncts your natal sun. A solunar chart is effective from one solunar Moon to the next solunar Moon. When you set up a solunar chart, you need to start with natal data—whether for yourself, your client, a business or place, or the location of an event. I set up my solunar charts as a bi-wheel, with the solunar in the center and the natal chart in the outer wheel. You could even set up your charts as a tri-wheel. I suggest that you put the solunar in the center, the natal in the second wheel, then the outer wheel could be a progression, or whatever you want. As with any chart work in astrology, I cannot emphasis enough the importance of using accurate data.

Following are the steps to set up a solunar chart using astrology software that is popular today.

Set up a solunar return in Solar Fire Gold, (version 7)

1. Enter the natal data.

2. Choose "Return & Ingress" from the Chart menu.

3. Change the place to the location for the applicable person, business, or event for which you want the solunar chart.

4. In the "Chart Type to Generate" box, select Advanced & Ingress.

5. Click the "Options" button.

6. From the scrollable list of selections, click on Sun, then in the "Return the Sun To" section of the screen, click the "Positions or Ingress" radio button. That will display the position of the natal Sun.

7. Next, click on Moon in the scrollable list of selections, then click OK to return to the main window.

8. Select "BiWheel" from the View menu.

9. With "Inner Wheel" highlighted in the Selected Charts list, click on the "Return"(the Moon Transiting" chart in the Charts list.

10. With "Outer Wheel" highlighted in the Selected Charts list, click on the "Natal" chart in the Charts list.

11. Click the View button to see your chart.

Set up a solunar return in Kepler (Sirius 1.1)

1. Enter the natal data.

2. From the toolbar below the menu, click on the "R" button, then select "Planet return."

3. In the "Location for the planet return" text field, enter the location for the applicable person, business, or event for which you want the solunar chart.

4. In the "Transiting planet" list, select Moon. In the "Natal planet" list, select Sun.

5. Click the OK button.

6. Choose "BiWheel" from the Wheel menu.

7. In the "Chart in the Inner Ring" list, select "Planet Return."

8. In the "Chart in the Outer Ring" list, select "Natal."

9. Click the OK button to see your chart.

Set up a solunar return in Matrix (WinStar 4.0)

1. Enter the natal data.

2. Click the "Return" button and select "Enter chart data"

3. Enter data

4. Run a solar chart

5. Run a lunar off of the solar chart to get the solunar

Interpreting the solunar chart

Once you have set up your solunar chart, it is time to interpret it. A solunar chart never stands alone—it is always run in conjunction with another chart, such as a natal or progressed chart. You might find it helpful to print out separate natal and solunar charts to compare with your bi-wheel.

This book was written based on a presentation to astrologers who have a working knowledge of delineating charts and a thorough understanding of house. If you are new to astrology, make sure you have your favorite reference book handy to look up information about the interpretations of planets and houses and how the sign will show how a planet will manifest its energy. Also keep in mind that the houses and the inter-relationship of derived houses are equally important. This can bring to light other persons or things represented by the houses.

Following are some important points to consider as you interpret your solunar chart. Note that when we mention planets, we also include other points such as Midheaven, Ascendant, vertex, antiscians, etc. Remember that not each month will be eventful. It may just be setting the stage for an active month ahead.

- **Solunar house.** Note the house of the solunar moon, which shows the beginning of your solunar month. The beginning of the solunar month is where the transiting moon conjuncts the natal sun.

- **Solunar Ascendant.** The first house is the solunar Ascendant (if you set up your chart with the solunar on the inside wheel). The sign of the solunar Ascendant sets up the conditions for that month. Note the planet that rules the solunar Ascendant, and where that planet is in the solunar and natal charts. An early degree rising on the Ascendant is indicative of a new beginning. A late degree rising may indicate that matters from the previous month are being completed.

- **Cusp signs.** When the signs of the solunar chart cusps are the same as the signs of natal cusps, this indicates a very active and important month.

- **New and full Moons.** Referring to an ephemeris or astrology reference software, add the locations on the chart of the monthly new and full Moons. The monthly new Moon is the conjunction of the Sun and Moon and is when you should begin preparing for new things. As the Moon progresses from new to full, the waxing phase, this continues the process of developing events for the month. The monthly full Moon is when the Moon reaches the opposition of the monthly new Moon and marks the beginning of the waning phase. This is the time to work through the things that you began at the monthly new Moon. The waning phase completes the cycle when it returns to the next monthly new Moon to begin a new monthly cycle.

- **Eclipses**. Mark solar and lunar eclipses on your chart. Because the effects of a solar eclipse can last for one year or more, mark a solar eclipse on your chart even if it occurred many months before. The energies of the houses that the eclipses fall across are intensified, as are the planets in those houses and any aspects to those planets.

- **Planets**. Look at the planets in the solunar chart, noting the houses they are in, their relationships with house rulers, and the aspects that they have with other planets. Consider whether planets are retrograde, direct, or on station. The degree at which a planet changes direction will remain sensitive until it changes direction again. Finally, note intercepted houses, as the planets involved may be held back.

- **Nodes**. Note any planets that are in the same degree as the nodes, as their energies will be particularly intense.

- **Aspects**. Check for aspects forming during the month and pay particular attention when the ruler of an angle is on an angle. One thing to consider about aspects is to use only applying aspects, as the separating aspects are left over from the previous month. Another thing to look for is whether a natal planet is conjunct a solunar angle, as this will bring the energy of that planet to the forefront for the month. Another meaningful aspect, and one which I think is major, is the *inconjunct* also called a *quincunx*. It has the energy of Uranus: sudden, unexpected, and needs readjusting and realigning as the two planets involved are always incompatible elements. An inconjunct can refer to a health problem or to the end, or death—not necessarily of a person but of an event.

- **Chart position.** When the solunar Moon and most of the planets fall on the eastern or left side of your chart (from the 10th to the 3rd houses), this is referred to as an active return and you have more freedom and are able to initiate personal choices. When the solunar chart has most of the planets on the western or right side of your chart (from the 4th to the 9th houses) you have less control and respond to the initiation of others. This is referred to as a reactive return. Planets above the horizon (from the 7th to 12th houses) are out in the open or are more likely to be externally expressed, while those below the horizon (from the 1st to 6th houses) are private, or more likely to be internally expressed.

- **Vertex.** The vertex is a very important point that should not be overlooked. Charles Jayne, an astrologer who has done considerable research on the vertex says: "The vertex is the most fated part of the horoscope." It attracts fateful encounters that can be karmic in nature.

  The vertex always falls on the western side of the chart. Where the vertex is there is action, the anti-vertex is just opposite the vertex on the eastern side of the chart, and it indicates what you put into motion to cause the reaction of the vertex. Charles Jayne has given the following formula to calculate this axis:

  > "Subtract the latitude of the birth place from 90 degrees in order to obtain the co-latitude. Use the IC (4th house cusp) as if it were the Midheaven, find that degree in the Table of Houses and go down to the co-latitude that you just figured. Whatever is listed there for the Ascendant becomes the vertex point. The opposite point (180 degrees away) is the anti-vertex, however most software programs will calculate the vertex."

- **Antiscia.** Antiscia points (solstice points) are hidden aspects which add another dimension to your interpretation and can be helpful when comparing charts. For each planet that is activated by an eclipse, an aspect, or something else, look to that planet's antiscia to see additional subtleties that have been exposed. This may be particularly evident concerning the Ascendant, Midheaven, Sun, and Moon. Remember that antiscian points for your solunar chart are only in effect for one month.

  To find an antiscia, note the sign the planet is in, then subtract the position of the planet from 29:60. Then use the table below to see what sign it is in. For example, my Sun is in 14 Gemini 26. To find the antiscia of my sun, I subtract 14:26 from 29:60 to get 15:34. Next I look at the table and see that the antiscia for Gemini is Cancer. So the antiscian point for my sun, is 15 Cancer 34.

The following table shows the Antiscians for each of the signs

Aries	→	Virgo	Libra	→	Pisces
Taurus	→	Leo	Scorpio	→	Aquarius
Gemini	→	Cancer	Sagittarius	→	Capricorn
Cancer	→	Gemini	Capricorn	→	Sagittarius
Leo	→	Taurus	Aquarius	→	Scorpio
Virgo	→	Aries	Pisces	→	Libra

- **Natural wheel**. Consider the qualities, elements, and polarities of the solunar moon. Refer to the chart on page 9 for a wheel which shows these attributes.

- **Critical degrees.** Always note critical degrees (0°, 13°, and 26°) of the cardinal signs: Aries, Cancer, Libra, and Capricorn. Note 9° and 21° of the fixed signs: Taurus, Leo, Scorpio, and Aquarius. And note 4° and 17° of the mutable signs: Gemini, Virgo, Sagittarius, and Pisces. These are always 13 degrees apart. Critical degrees operate adversely, bringing matters to a head, denoting a crisis, and adding an emphasis to any planet they touch.

- **Turn the chart.** Turn the chart to get additional information. This method, used in solar astrology, turns the chart so that the Sun (and in this case the solunar Moon) is used as the Ascendant. This technique is called turning the chart, derived houses, or "wheels within wheels." Note when interpreting the Ascendant ruler after you have turned the chart, the same natal planet must be considered. For example, if Mercury is the solunar Ascendant ruler, observe where natal Mercury falls in the chart.

- **Other points.** You may also use Arabic parts, progressions, declinations, or any special degree such as prenatal eclipse, etc. For example, my prenatal eclipse degree is 14° Pisces, so any month when that degree is prominent on my chart I know something important will happen.

Using solunar charts for timing
Your solunar chart is excellent for timing events. Using an ephemeris or your astrology reference software, write the degrees and dates where the transiting Moon enters each house.

On the hour that the transiting moon conjuncts a planet, this is when events involving the energies of that planet are most likely to occur. It is particularly important to note the time the transiting Moon conjuncts your Ascendant and the ruler of your

Ascendant. Also note the antiscias when you work on timing. You may mark in advance the days of importance to watch or days to schedule events. And finally, it is important to note that you can progress the chart one degree a day.

Borrowing from a horary rule, the last aspect the Moon makes before leaving the sign can be very telling on how the month will end.

Natural chart

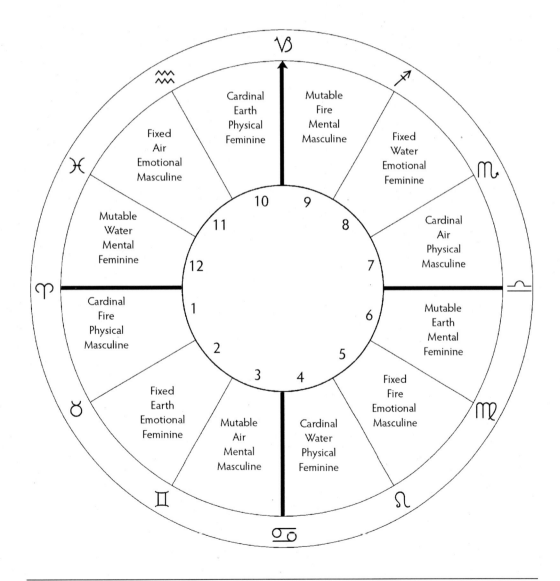

Astrological glyphs

Almost all the charts in this book are accompanied by numbered notes indicating areas of particular interest. The charts and the notes are written using classic astrological glyphs, as shown below. In the chart notes, the superscripted symbol "N" specifies items from the natal chart, "P" for items from progressed charts, "SL" for items from the solunar chart, and "T" for items which are transiting. OOB means "out of bounds."

Signs		Planets/Positions		Aspects/Directions	
♈	Aries	☉	Sun	☌	Conjunct
♉	Taurus	☽	Moon	☍	Opposition
♊	Gemini	⊗	Earth	□	Square
♋	Cancer	☿	Mercury	∠	Semisquare
♌	Leo	♀	Venus	⚎	Sesquare
♍	Virgo	♂	Mars	⚻	Inconjunct
♎	Libra	♃	Jupiter	‖	Parallel
♏	Scorpio	♄	Saturn	⚌	Contraparallel
♐	Sagittarius	♅	Uranus	△	Trine
♑	Capricorn	♆	Neptune	✶	Sextile
♒	Aquarius	♇	Pluto	⩛	Semisextile
♓	Pisces	Vx	Vertex	Q	Quintile
		MC	Midheaven	℞	Retrograde
		Asc	Ascendant		

The font used in this book for the astrological symbols is available from RightLeft Graphics at www.rightleftgraphics.com.

9/11 Terrorist Attack

First we will look at the charts for an event that had a major impact on history in the United States and the world: the terrorist attack of September 11, 2001.

The coordinated attacks of 9/11 resulted in the deaths of 2,993 people, including people in and near the attacked buildings, rescuers, passengers on the planes involved, and 19 terrorists. We will look at charts for the World Trade Center and the Pentagon.

World Trade Center

First we will look at the natal chart of the World Trade Center in New York City. Particularly focus on two things about this chart: the Ascendant at 0° Leo, and the vertex at 15° Sagittarius. I use the vertex a lot because it tells you many things.

Natal Chart, World Trade Center
Time: April 4, 1973 (Wednesday), 12:00 p.m. EST +5:00
Location: New York, NY, USA 40°N42'51" 074°W00'23"

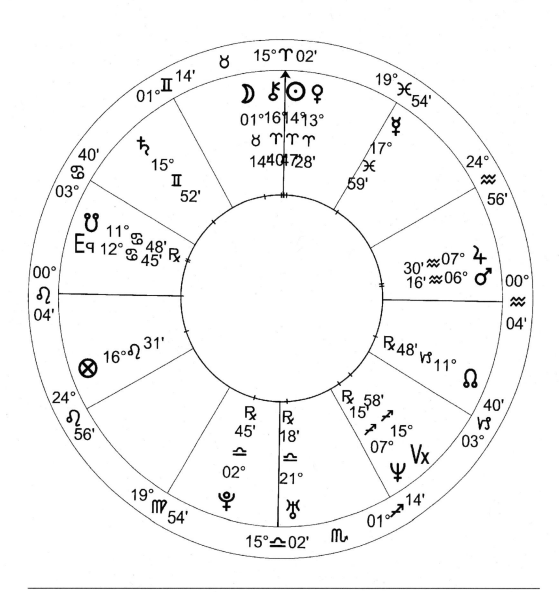

Next look at solunar of the World Trade Center for September 5, 2001, which is when the transiting Moon conjuncted the natal Sun in the 4th house.

Note the natal vertex on the Ascendant of the World Trade Center, and the natal Ascendant on the solunar vertex. With these aspects, you know something is going on. Now take the transiting Moon as it enters each house and note the date that it enters the house. Look at September 12 when the Moon entered – actually it entered on the September 11 between September 10 and September 12 on the chart in the 7th house.

Other aspects to note are solunar Saturn at 15° Gemini opposite the Ascendant at 16° Sagittarius, with the natal vertex at 16° Sagittarius and Pluto at 13° Sagittarius squaring the natal Sun and the Saturn/Pluto midpoint. The Part of Disaster is 15° Pisces 46 opposite the solunar Sun and squaring the Ascendant, Pluto, and Saturn. For those who follow declinations, Mars was out of bounds (-26°56'), which means it was beyond the limits of the Sun and does not follow the Sun's rules. Also note the square of the natal Sun at 13° Virgo, the square Saturn, and the Part of Disaster was at 13° Virgo. Notice the intercepted 3rd and 9th houses.

The following notes refer to the numbered arrows on the chart:

①	^{SL}☽ ☌ ^{N}☉ in 4th house
②	^{N}Asc ☌ ^{SL}Vx
③	♄/♀ = 13° ♍ 46' ☌ ^{SL}☉
④	^{SL}Asc ☌ ^{N}Vx
⑤	^{N}♂ ruler of 4th house (OOB -26°56') ☌ ^{SL}♆ ☍ ♀ ruler of MC
⑥	^{SL}Part of Death = 15° ♓ 35' □ 1/7 house ☍ ^{SL}☉

INNER WHEEL: Solunar Chart, World Trade Center, Moon Transiting 14° ♈ 47'07"
Time: September 5, 2001 (Wednesday), 2:23:30 p.m. EDT +4:00
Location: Manhattan, NY, USA 40°N46' 073°W59'

OUTER WHEEL: Natal Chart, World Trade Center
Time: April 4, 1973 (Wednesday), 12:00 p.m. EST +5:00
Location: New York, NY, USA 40°N42'51" 074°W00'23"

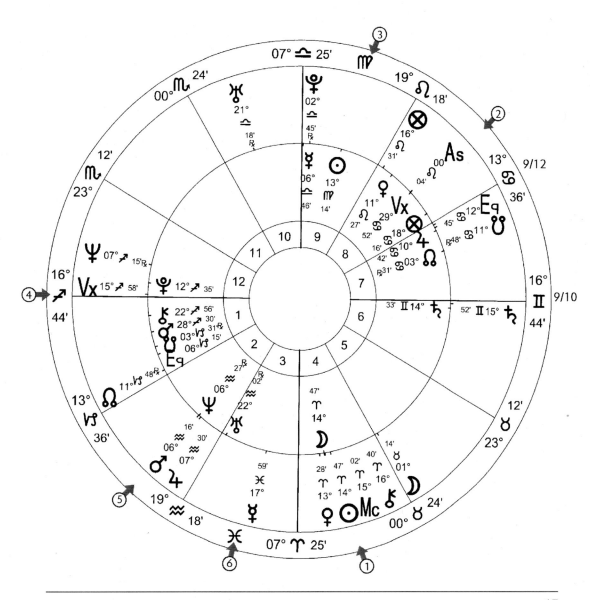

Pentagon

Now let's look at the charts for the Pentagon. The first chart is the natal chart of the Pentagon from Astro-Databank (www.astro.com/astro-databank/). Notice the intercepted 4th and 10th houses.

The following note refers to the numbered arrow on the chart:

①   ᴾ☽ = 28° ♐ ♂ Part of Fortune

Natal Chart, Pentagon
Time: April 29, 1942 (Wednesday), 10:30 a.m. EWT +4:00
Location: Washington, DC, USA 38°N53'42" 077°W02'12"

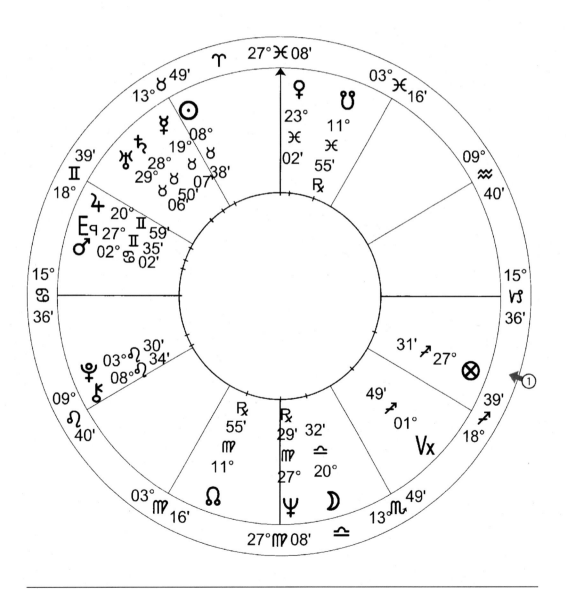

Let's look at the progressed chart for the Pentagon. I progress these charts to see if there's anything happening. Note the progressed Moon is inconjunct Uranus, ruler of the 7th house, and inconjunct Venus, ruler of the Midheaven. The Ascendant is 29° Leo. Notice the intercepted 10th and 4th houses.

The following notes refer to the numbered arrows on the chart:

①	ᴾ☽ ⚻ ♀ ruler of the MC and ⚻ ♅ ruler of the 7th house
②	Asc at 29° Leo

Progressed Chart, Pentagon
Time: September 11, 2001 (Tuesday), 8:04 a.m. EWT +4:00
Location: Washington, DC, USA 38°N53'42" 077°W02'12"

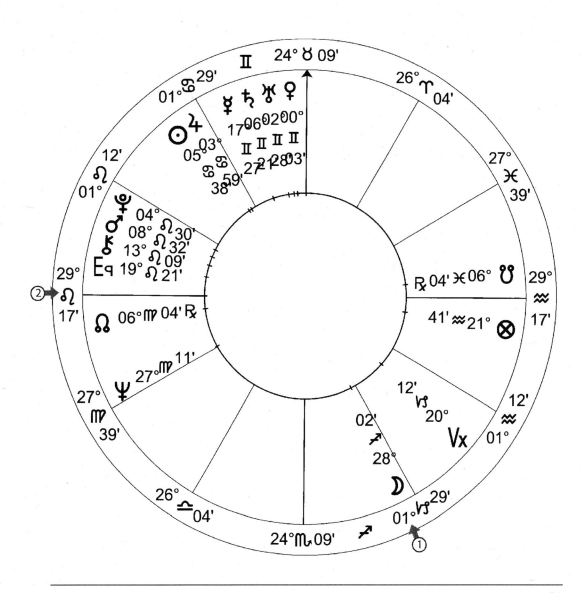

Now look at the chart for September 7, 2001. The solunar Ascendant at 0° Sagittarius is conjunct the natal vertex. The solunar Moon is in the 6th house.

If you start using the vertex, you will be amazed at what you can find out. The natal vertex is on the solunar Ascendant, the natal Ascendant is on solunar vertex in the 8th house, and natal Uranus is on the solunar 7th house opposite solunar Ascendant. What else do we see here – there's September 11, exactly when that was triggered off. We have a natal T-square between the Sun, Pluto, and Saturn ready for a trigger. Now along comes the solunar Midheaven that triggers the event.

Of course we've had the same midpoint applying since it only happened minutes later, with the very same midpoints going on of disaster, violence, and so forth—which certainly describes what happened at that time.

The following notes refer to the numbered arrows on the chart:

①	^{SL}☽ ♂ ^{N}☉ in the 6th house
②	^{N}♅ on the ^{SL}7th house
③	^{N}ASC ♂ ^{SL}Vx in the 8th house
④	^{SL}ASC ♂ ^{N}Vx
⑤	^{P}☽ = 28° ♐ ♂ ^{SL}♂ ⊼ ^{N}♅ and ^{N}♄

INNER WHEEL: Solunar Chart, Pentagon, Moon Transiting 08° ♉ 38'
Time: September 7, 2001 (Friday), 1:03:13 p.m. EDT +4:00
Location: Washington, DC, USA 38°N52'15" 077°W03'23"

OUTER WHEEL: Natal Chart, Pentagon
Time: April 29, 1942 (Wednesday), 10:30 a.m. EWT +4:00
Location: Washington, DC, USA 38°N53'42" 077°W02'12"

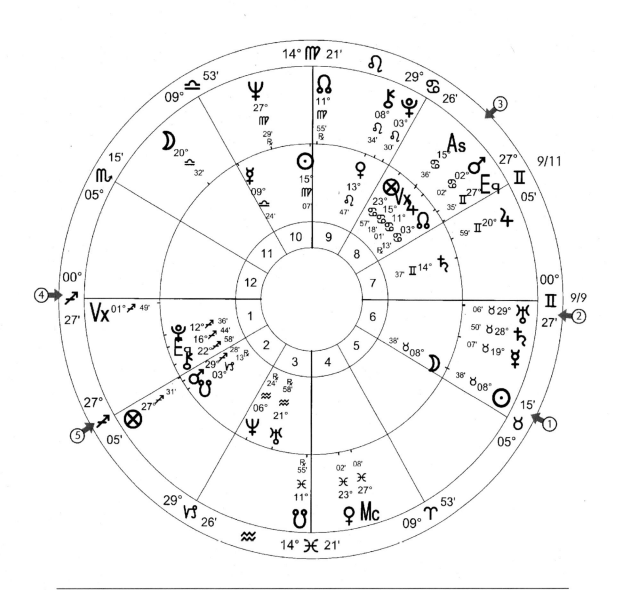

Christopher Reeve

We'll turn now from events to people and the events in their lives. I have always been fascinated with the actor Christopher Reeve.

Christopher D'Olier Reeve was an American actor, director, and screenwriter, known chiefly for his iconic role in the Superman films in the 1980s. He became a quadriplegic in 1995 after being thrown from his horse, and quickly became a strong and influential voice on behalf of spinal cord injury victims and in support of embryonic stem cell research.

I have followed his life right along and have run charts for different phases of his life.

Let's look at his natal chart. I wanted you to see this chart because eclipses are excellent timers, and there was an eclipse in April 1995 at 9° Taurus on his Midheaven.

The following notes refer to the numbered arrows on the chart:

   ①   Eclipse April 25, 1995 at 9° ♉ ♂ MC

Natal Chart, Christopher Reeve
Time: September 25, 1952 (Thursday), 3:12 a.m. EDT +4:00
Location: New York, NY, USA 40°N42'51" 074°W00'23"

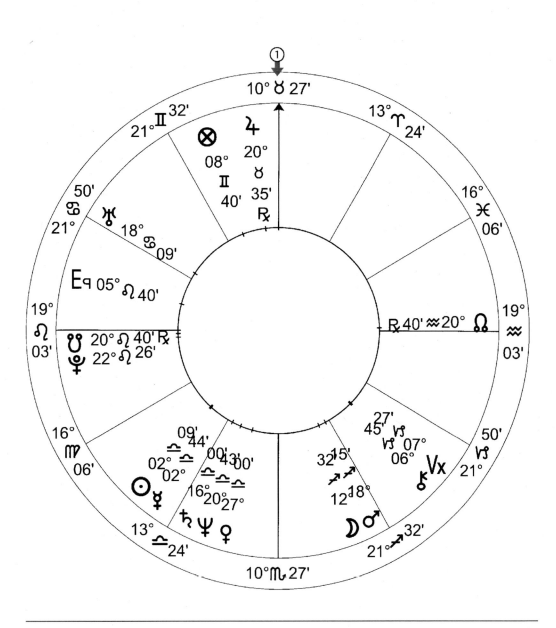

In 1995 Christopher Reeve was profoundly injured when he was thrown from his horse. In the accident chart, the solunar Moon is in the 6th house.

On the day of the accident, the transiting Moon was 18° Taurus, approaching the natal Jupiter and solunar Sun in the 2nd house. His progressed Ascendant was 23° Virgo, opposing the solunar Saturn in the 12th house (chart not shown).

I always show the new and full Moons in the chart. In the accident chart, the full Moon is at 23° Scorpio on May 14, and solunar Pluto is at 29° in the 8th house. Look on the 7th house cusp where the natal Mercury conjuncts the solunar vertex, conjuncting the Moon. Also solunar Mars is at 24° Leo, inconjuncts Saturn in the 12th house, and conjuncts natal Pluto, the south node, and the Ascendant. Notice the intercepted 6th and 12th houses.

The following notes refer to the numbered arrows on the chart:

①	^{SL}☽ ☌ ^{N}☉ in the 6th house
②	^{N}☿ 3° ♎ (OOB+24° 40) ☌ ^{SL}Vx □ Mc
③	Full☽ May14 at 23° ♏
④	^{N}♂ ruler of Asc and co-ruler of 8th house □ ^{SL}♄
⑤	Antiscia of ^{SL}Asc 23° ♍ in the 6th house intercepted
⑥	^{T}☽ 18° ♉ @1:30 p.m. with ♂/♀ midpoint 20° ♉
⑦	^{N}♃ ☌ ^{SL}☉ ⊼ ^{N}♆ with ♂/♀ midpoint 20° ♉
⑧	^{SL}♂ 24° ♌ ⊼ ♄ in the 12th house, ruler of the MC ^{SL}♂ ☌ ^{N}♀, ☋, and Asc
⑨	^{P}Asc (from the progressed chart, not shown) 23° ♍ ☍ ^{SL}♄, Antiscia of ^{SL}Asc=23° ♍ in the 6th house intercepted

INNER WHEEL: Solunar Chart, Christopher Reeve, Moon Transiting 02° ♎ 9'21"
Time: May 11, 1995 (Thursday), 4:13:50 a.m. EDT +4:00
Location: Culpeper, VA, USA 38°N28'23" 077°W59'

OUTER WHEEL: Natal Chart, Christopher Reeve
Time: September 25, 1952 (Thursday), 3:12 a.m. EDT +4:00
Location: New York, NY, USA 40°N42'51" 074°W00'23"

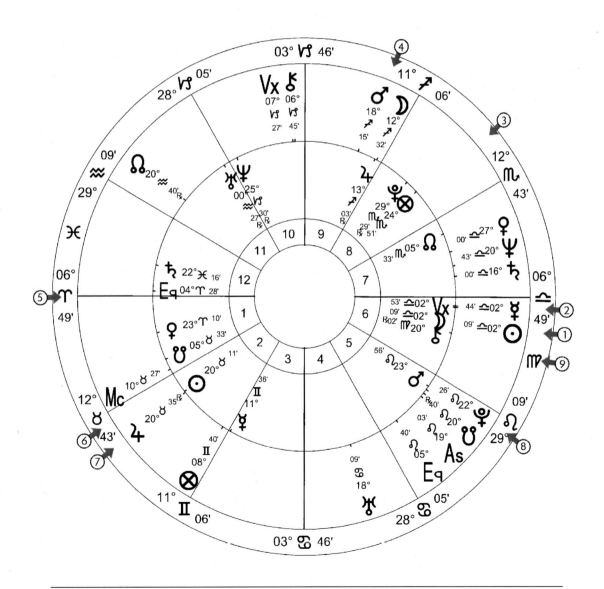

Just nine years after the accident, Christopher Reeve died. In the progressed chart for the day that he died, his natal Part of Death was 22° Scorpio 39'. You see his progressed Sun at 23° Scorpio 55' in the 4th house, squaring natal Pluto and the south node in the 1st house. His progressed Ascendant is conjuncting his natal Sun, and his progressed Moon is at the 4th house cusp – the end of life.

The following notes refer to the numbered arrows on the chart:

①	ᴾ☽ ♂ the 4th house cusp
②	ᴾ☉ 23° ♏ 55' in the 4th house ☐ ᴺ☋, ☊, and ♀ Part of Death=22° ♏ 39' ♂ ᴾ☉, ☐ 1st and 7th houses and ☐ ♀, ☍ ᴺ♃
③	ᴾ☋ ♂ Asc and ♂ ᴾ♀ ☐ ᴾ☉
④	ᴾAsc ♂ ᴺ☉

INNER WHEEL: Natal Chart, Christopher Reeve
Time: September 25, 1952 (Thursday), 3:12 a.m. EDT +4:00
Location: New York, NY, USA 40°N42'51" 074°W00'23"

OUTER WHEEL: Secondary Progressed Chart, Christopher Reeve
Time: October 10, 2004 (Sunday), 3:12 a.m. EDT +4:00
Location: New York, NY, USA 40°N42'51" 074°W00'23"

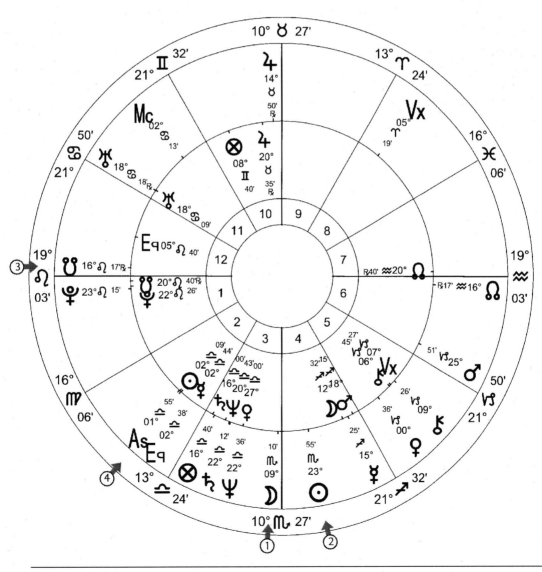

Next is the chart which shows his death.

Zeros can be very significant in a chart–whether they're new beginnings, transitions, or endings. Christopher Reeve died on October 10, 2004 when the transiting Moon was exactly on his Ascendant. The eclipse of October 13, 2004 was at 21° Libra on his natal Neptune.

Another important thing to notice is the solunar Moon is conjunct Mercury, ruler of the Ascendant. This was the solunar that took place September 15 in his 2nd house, and by the time the Moon reached the Ascendant at 0° Virgo, he passed from this life.

The following notes refer to the numbered arrows on the chart:

①	^{SL}☽ ☌ ^{N}☉ in the 2nd house ☌ ♀
②	Eclipse October 13, 2004 @ 21° ♎ ☌ ^{N}♆ □ ^{SL}♄ and Vx
③	^{N}Part of Death = 22° ♏ 39' ☌ 4th house cusp (end of matter)
④	Asc at 0° ♍, also ^{T}☽ on Asc

INNER WHEEL: Solunar Chart, Christopher Reeve, Moon Transiting 02° ♎ 9'21"
Time: September 15, 2004 (Wednesday), 4:48:04 a.m. EDT +4:00
Location: New York, NY, USA 40°N42'51" 074°W00'23"

OUTER WHEEL: Natal Chart, Christopher Reeve
Time: September 25, 1952 (Thursday), 3:12 a.m. EDT +4:00
Location: New York, NY, USA 40°N42'51" 074°W00'23"

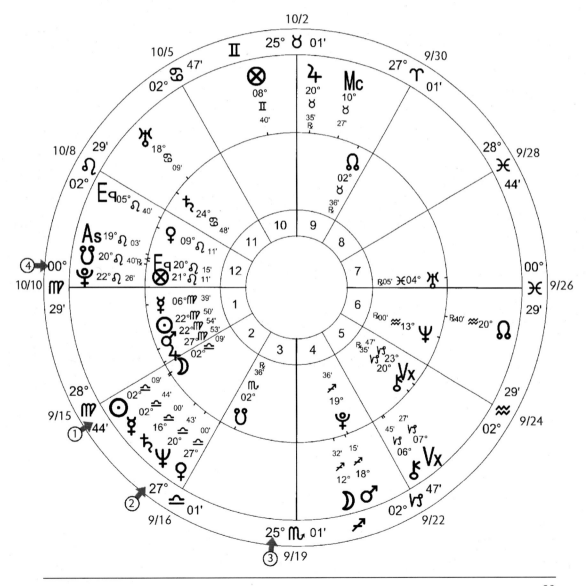

Michael Jackson

Another influential figure in the entertainment industry is Michael Jackson.

A very controversial figure, Michael Joseph Jackson was known as the King of Pop. He was an entertainment star from early in his life with the Jackson Five, and later made a name for himself with his solo work and innovative dancing.

Dietrech Pessin has Michael Jackson's chart in her book *Lunar Shadows*. Dietrech delineated the chart and it was very accurate for what she was showing. Virginia Reyer had a completely different chart in an article she wrote for *Considerations*, which she rectified based on her research on Michael Jackson. Even though the charts were different due to a difference in the birth time, they both worked.

With a solunar return, can we see which one more closely fits Michael?

This chart is the one from *Lunar Shadows*. It seemed like Michael Jackson, with Scorpio rising and the Moon in Pisces in the 4th house.

In this chart (Michael Jackson #1), the vertex is on the Ascendant, the natal Moon is conjuncting the Midheaven, and the natal Ascendant is conjuncting the solunar vertex. We have got the solunar at 5° Virgo on the 4th house cusp (his natal Sun is 5° Virgo). When you have the Sun/Pluto or Sun/Saturn midpoints, you know it's time to make a decision, especially with the solunar in the 3rd house. He was acquitted of child molestation charges on June 13, 2005 at 2:14 p.m. PDT, and this chart shows a Sun/Pluto opposition.

The following notes refer to the numbered arrows on the chart:

①	^{SL}☽ ☌ ^{N}☉ in the 3rd house ☌ 4th house cusp, end of matter
②	☉/♀ midpoint 22° ♍ 54' □ ^{SL}☉ ☍ ♀ ⊼ ^{SL}☊ and ⊼ ^{N}☋
③	☉/♄ 27° ♎ ☌ ^{N}♃, △ Asc
④	^{SL}Vx ☌ ^{N}Asc
⑤	^{N}☽ ☌ ^{SL}MC and ^{SL}♅
⑥	^{SL}☉ ☍ ♀ □ ☉/♀ midpoint @ 22° ♍ 54' in 4th house
⑦	^{SL}Asc ☌ ^{N}Vx
⑧	♀/♀ midpoint 24° ♌ ☌ ^{N}MC and ☿ ruler of Asc and the 4th house

INNER WHEEL: Solunar Chart, Michael Jackson (#1), Moon Transiting 05° ♍ 50'44"
Time: June 13, 2005 (Monday), 6:08:24 a.m. PDT +7:00
Location: Santa Maria, CA, USA 34°N57'11" 120°W26'05"

OUTER WHEEL: Natal Chart, Michael Jackson (#1)
Time: August 29, 1958 (Friday), 12:09 p.m. CDT +5:00
Location: Gary, IN, USA 41°N35'36" 087°W20'47"

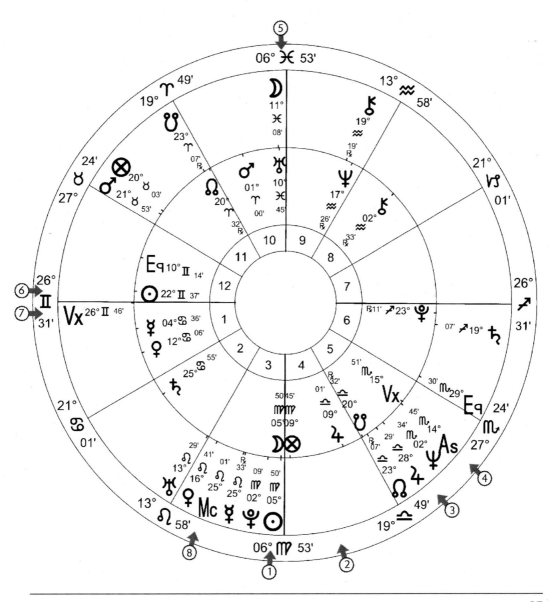

The next chart is from Virginia Reyer's article. Because the Moon has traveled six degrees, we know it had to be a difference of close to 12 hours.

In this chart (Michael Jackson #2), it just so happened that the solunar came due on the day of the decision, and we have the Sun/Saturn midpoint exactly on the solunar Ascendant. We have natal Venus/Pluto midpoint at 24° Leo on his natal Mercury and opposing the natal Midheaven (remember the outside wheel is the natal chart). We have Sun/Pluto midpoint at 22° Pisces, exactly on the Midheaven.

Be sure to note the natal vertex to the Ascendant. I started paying attention to the vertex many years ago, and I really know that it works. The vertex is a fated point in the chart – it's known as a third angle. It always appears on the Libra side of the chart, where other people have an influence on your life. The anti-vertex is exactly opposite: it's what you set into motion that causes the reaction on the other side.

I have one example that I use all the time: the Saturn age arc. When I ran Bill Clinton's chart, his vertex is in the 7th house and by age arc, it became active when he was about 16 years old, which is when his high school class toured the White House and he shook the hand of JFK. He has said that handshake was when he decided to go into politics. I always use that example of someone coming along and, not changing your destiny, but having an influence on your life. Notice the intercepted 10th and 4th houses.

The following notes refer to the numbered arrows on the chart:

①	$^{SL}\mathrm{☽}$ ♂ $^{N}\mathrm{☉}$ in the 3rd house
②	$^{N}\mathrm{☽}$ ♂ $^{SL}\mathrm{MC}$, ☽ rules $^{SL}\mathrm{Asc}$
③	☉/♀ midpoint 22° ♓ ♂ MC
④	$^{N}\mathrm{Asc}$ coming to $^{SL}\mathrm{☉}$
⑤	$^{SL}\mathrm{☉}$ ☍ ♀ □ 4th/10th house cusps
⑥	$^{SL}\mathrm{☉}$/♄ midpoint 9° ♋ 17' on Asc
⑦	$^{N}\mathrm{♀}$ ☍ $^{SL}\mathrm{♆}$ in 8th house
⑧	$^{N}\mathrm{♀}$/♀ midpoint 24° ♌ 44' ♂ $^{N}\mathrm{☿}$ □ $^{SL}\mathrm{Vx}$

Note: Anne Vick passed away six months before Michael Jackson's June 2009 death, however she would have done his chart with the Solunars. Nelda Tanner, a friend and colleague of Anne's and who edited this book, has provided additional charts that show Michael Jackson's death. See "Solunar Chart Workshop" on pagepage 89.

INNER WHEEL: Solunar Chart, Michael Jackson (#2), Moon Transiting 06° ♍ 19'04"
Time: June 13, 2005 (Monday), 7:05:20 a.m. PDT +7:00
Location: Santa Maria, CA, USA 34°N57'11" 120°W26'05"

OUTER WHEEL: Natal Chart, Michael Jackson (#2)
Time: August 29, 1958 (Friday), 11:53 p.m. CDT +5:00
Location: Gary, IN, USA 41°N35'36" 087°W20'47"

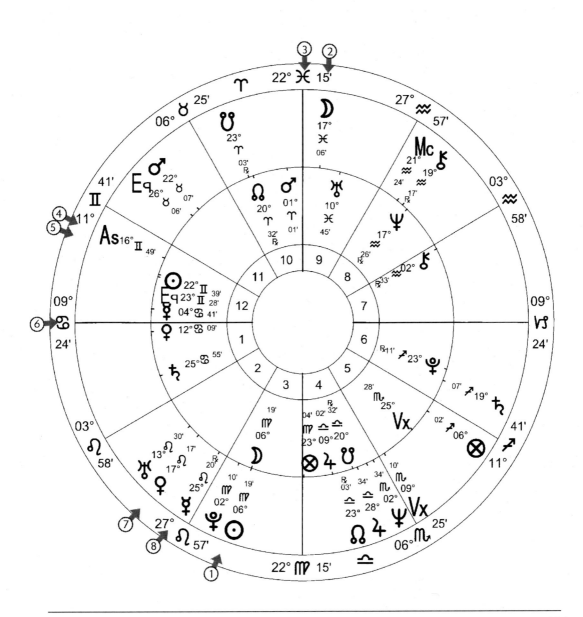

Pope John Paul

From influential men in entertainment, we turn to men of the Church. Next we will look at the solunar chart for Pope John Paul and the assassination attempt of 1981.

Pope John Paul II was born Karol Jozef Wójtyla in Poland. The second longest reigning Pope, he served as the Pope of the Catholic Church for nearly 27 years.

The attempted assassination occurred when Pope John Paul was touring Rome on May 13, 1981 at 5:21:31 p.m.

The solunar is in his 2nd house, as is the vertex. I don't mean to keep pushing the vertex, but you'll catch on. The solunar opposes Uranus. Now if you were the Pope's astrologer, would you have given him any warning? Look at his natal Mars conjunct Pluto. I mean it can't be that good. His natal Ascendant is 5 degrees from Pluto, but it inconjuncts his solunar at 27° Taurus – that's the degree of the Sun.

This chart shows solunar Uranus opposing the natal Sun at 27° Taurus, and natal Mars conjunct Pluto. Solunar Mercury and the Moon are inconjunct Neptune at 24° Sagittarius and the Midheaven. His natal Ascendant and Mars are also conjuncting Pluto. Look at the solunar Midheaven at 24° Sagittarius.

It is also interesting to look at the antiscians, which are mirror images and crisis points. The antiscian of his Midheaven 5° Capricorn 59' and is opposing natal Pluto within 1 minute. So how lucky could he be? Do you think this was a good day for him to be out there?

As a side note, the fixed star nearest 27° Taurus is Algol, which is at 26° Taurus and is said to be the Demon Star. Also Saturn and Pluto are in the 7th house of open enemies. There is also a yod in effect, with Neptune sextiling Pluto, and both of them inconjuncting natal Venus and Mercury. I did the chart for the exact time of the attempted assassination, and the chart is pretty accurate.

The following notes refer to the numbered arrows on the chart:

①	ᔆᴸ☽ ☌ ᴺ☉ in the 2nd house ☌ ᴺVx ☍ ᔆᴸ♅ in 8th house
②	ᔆᴸ☿ and ☽ ⚻ ♆ at the MC
③	ᵀ☽ 5/13 = 23° ♍ 55' ☌ ᔆᴸVx in 7th house
④	ᴺ♂ ☌ ᔆᴸ♀ (in yod)
⑤	ᴺAsc ⚻ ᴺ☉ and ᔆᴸ☽
⑥	Antiscia of MC 23°♐ 55' = 5° ♑ 59' ☍ ᴺ♀ in 4th house
Part of Death 18° ♎ 58' in the 7th house ☌ ᴺ♂ and ᔆᴸ♀	
Part of Danger or Peril 07° ♋ 10' ☌ ᴺ♀	
Part of Fatality 04° ♒ 49' ☌ ᔆᴸ☋, ☍ ᴺMC	
Part of Catastrophe 05° ♌ 22' ☌ ᴺMC and ᔆᴸ☊	

INNER WHEEL: Solunar Chart, Pope John Paul, Moon Transiting 27° ♉ 21'32"
Time: May 5, 1981 (Tuesday), 3:51:24 a.m. CEDT -2:00
Location: Rome, Italy 41°N54' 012°E29'

OUTER WHEEL: Natal Chart, Pope John Paul
Time: May 18, 1920 (Tuesday), 5:30 p.m. EET -2:00
Location: Wadowice, Poland 49°N53' 019°E30'

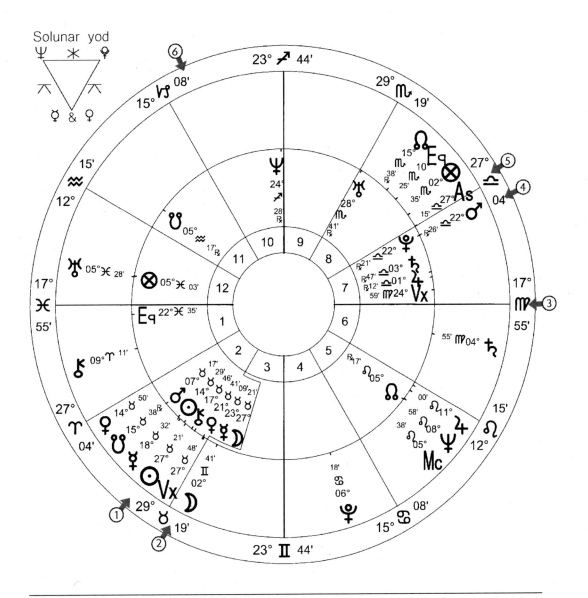

Solunar yod

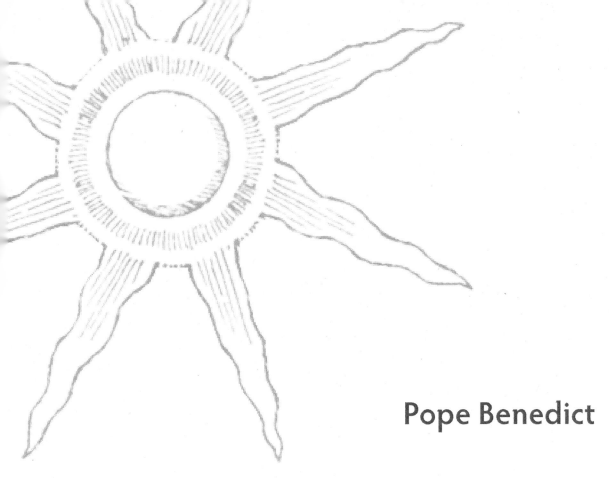

Pope Benedict

Now we will look at Pope Benedict XVI, the new guy on the block, showing his natal chart along with the chart for when he was elected.

He was born Joseph Alois Ratzinger in Bavaria and became the 265th reigning Pope of the Catholic Church.

Pope Benedict was elected on April 19, 2005 at 12:40 p.m. ET. When there are four or more planets in the same house, this is called a stellium. The solunar Moon is in the 11th house, as is the Aries stellium.

The natal Moon is conjunct the solunar Jupiter, intercepted on April 19. So the transiting Moon was probably just about on the Neptune, which trines his solunar. He's got a fire trine, a grand trine: solunar Pluto at 24° Sagittarius with natal Midheaven, the natal Sun at 25° Aries, and natal Neptune at 24° Leo. So he's certainly got everything he needs. His natal Pluto is 14° Cancer trine solunar Uranus in the 10th house.

The Neptunian influences in his chart and the grand trine are very appropriate for him being elected pope. Notice the intercepted 11th and 5th houses.

The following notes refer to the numbered arrows on the chart:

①	^{SL}☽ ☌ ^{N}☉ in the 11th house intercepted
②	^{N}♀ 14° Cancer △ ^{N}Asc in the 10th house and △ ^{SL}♅ ruler of the MC
③	^{T}☽ ☌ ^{N}♆ △ the stellium in the 11th house
④	^{N}☽ ☌ ^{SL}♃ intercepted in the 5th house △ ^{SL}♆ and the ^{SL}MC
⑤	^{SL}♆ ☌ MC ruling 11th house in mutual reception with ♅ in 10th house

INNER WHEEL: Solunar Chart, Pope Benedict, Moon Transiting 25° ♈ 08'43"
Time: April 9, 2005 (Saturday), 9:11:36 a.m. CEDT -2:00
Location: Vatican City, Italy 41°N54'   012°E27'

OUTER WHEEL: Natal Chart, Pope Benedict
Time: April 16, 1927 (Saturday), 4:15 a.m. CET -1:00
Location: Marktl, Germany 48°N15'   012°E51'

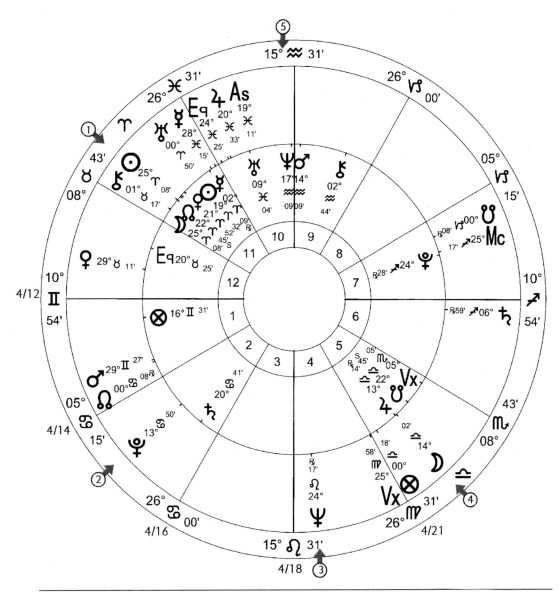

Sandra Day O'Conner

From the Church we turn to the Law. We will look at several charts for former U.S. Supreme Court Justice Sandra Day O'Conner.

Sandra Day O'Conner was the first female member of the Supreme Court of the United States starting in 1981. She is a very powerful woman and an inspiration to women around the world.

This is her natal chart, progressed to June 28, 2005, a few days before her July 1 announcement that she would retire from the Supreme Court. She was having a nodal return. There was an eclipse on April 8 at 19° Aries. Her progressed Midheaven is coming to her natal Ascendant, and her progressed Moon is at 28° Scorpio. Notice the intercepted 9th and 3rd houses.

The following notes refer to the numbered arrows on the chart:

①	ᴾ☽ 28° ♏ △ ᴺ☿ and the 4th house cusp (☿ ruler of the 7th house and intercepted 9th)
②	ᴾMC ♂ ᴺAsc
③	Eclipse on April 8, 2005 19° ♈ ♂ ᴺ♀ ruler of the 10th house
④	Nodal return

INNER WHEEL: Natal Chart, Sandra Day O'Conner
Time: March 26, 1930 (Wednesday), 00:22 a.m. MST +7:00
Location: Phoenix, AZ, USA 33°N26'54" 112°W04'24"

OUTER WHEEL: Secondary Progressed Chart, Sandra Day O'Conner
Time: June 28, 2005 (Tuesday), 10:30:21 a.m. MST +7:00
Location: Phoenix, AZ, USA 33°N26'54" 112°W04'24"

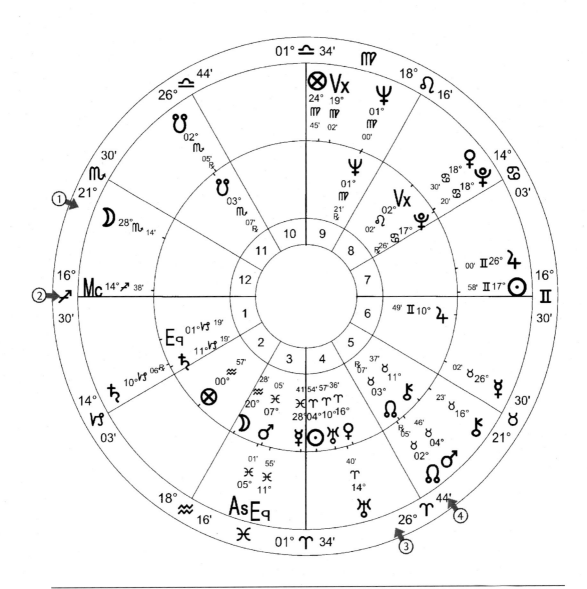

This is the day that her solunar came due. As I said before, you can progress the chart 1 degree per day. O'Conner's chart has 29° Taurus on the Midheaven, which indicates an ending of career, and two days later it was on her Part of Fortune. Her solunar took place on the 8th house—known as the release from personal obligations.

Her announcement was certainly sudden and unexpected, as shown by Uranus in the 7th house. The 10th house is at an ending degree and also at 29° Taurus, so there may have been some sadness that went along with making this decision to resign. You can see the benefit of using houses and knowing all your house interpretations.

Other things about her life at the time can be seen in this chart as well. Her natal Neptune on the solunar Ascendant can indicate an illness in the family. In fact, her husband has Alzheimer's.

If we look back at her progressed chart, the Moon is at 28° Scorpio 14' on her 4th house of endings, and the full Moon was 28° Capricorn opposing Saturn. That was actually on the 21st, but it's still active in this chart. Notice the intercepted 10th and 4th houses.

The following notes refer to the numbered arrows on the chart:

①	ᔆᴸ☽ ♂ ᴺ☉ in the 8th house
②	Eclipse April 8, 2005 19° ♈ ♂ ᴺ♀, ♂ ᔆᴸ☊
③	ᔆᴸMC = 29° ♉ ♂ ᔆᴸPart of Fortune
④	ᴺVx ♂ ᔆᴸ♀ and ☿ ruling MC, the 2nd house, Asc, and the intercepted 10th house
⑤	ᴺ♆ ♂ ᔆᴸAsc
⑥	ᴾ☽ 28° ♏ ♂ 4th house cusp
⑦	Full ☽ 28° ♑ on July 21 ☍ ᔆᴸ♄ △ ᔆᴸMC

INNER WHEEL: Solunar Chart, Sandra Day O'Conner , Moon Transiting 04° ♈ 54'38"
Time: June 28, 2005 (Tuesday), 10:27:38 a.m. EDT +4:00
Location: Washington, DC, USA (Supreme Court Building) 38°N53'26" 077°W00'17"

OUTER WHEEL: Natal Chart, Sandra Day O'Conner
Time: March 26, 1930 (Wednesday), 00:22 a.m. MST +7:00
Location: Phoenix, AZ, USA 33°N26'54" 112°W04'24"

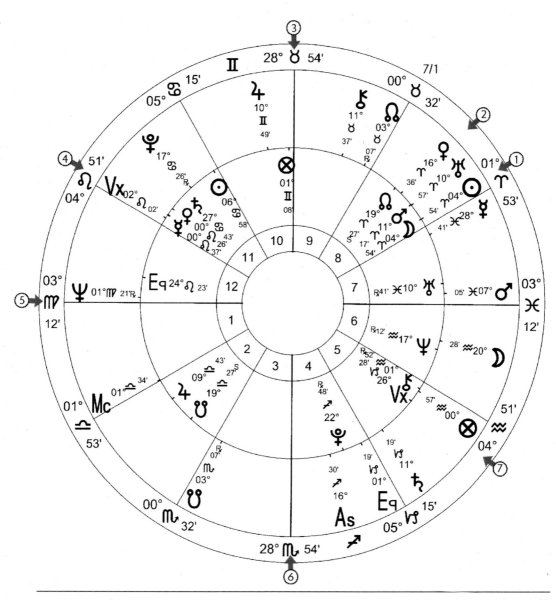

Terry Schiavo

What do you do when you haven't got a date of birth but you have an event date that you know is accurate? Terry Schiavo's chart is a good example of this problem.

Terry Schiavo collapsed from a cardiac arrest in February 1990. Although paramedics arrived on the scene and attempted to revive her, her brain had gone quite a long time without oxygen. This led to a brain injury and she was sustained by life support. Her husband fought a protracted and controversial legal battle against her parents for the right to have her removed from life support so her life could end.

I thought this would be a very interesting chart to see. I was able to get the place and the date of her birth, but I did not have an accurate time. I wasn't going to do solunars without an accurate time! But I did have an accurate time of her passing, so I ran the chart based on that.

Terry Schiavo died on March 31, 2005 at 9:05 a.m. EST. The solunar Moon is in the 9th house. Her natal Moon is inconjunct Saturn and coming to conjunct Pluto. There were quite a few aspects going on there.

The solunar that preceded her death was at 10° Aries 57'. Look at the Sun again in the 8th house—in fact her 8th house has a lot going on in it. The Midheaven of the event chart conjuncts the Neptune. The outer planets didn't change by much because it was only a matter of days – the solunar took place on the 11th, and on March 31 you can see again that was when the transiting Moon entered the 5th house, probably on the Pluto.

Neptune was in 3 degrees opposition the Ascendant. Now look in the other chart, where the Sun and the Moon are squaring each other. The Sun in the chart is at 21° Pisces squaring the Moon of the event at 21° Sagittarius. This makes me wonder if that was the husband and the parents and all the problems that they were having.

While it can be interesting to run a chart based on an event, it really is best to start with an accurate natal.

The following notes refer to the numbered arrows on the chart:

①	^{SL}☽ ☌ ^{N}☉ in the 9th house
②	^{N}♀ ☌ ^{SL}☽, ruler of MC and 12th house
③	^{N}☽ ⊼ ^{SL}♄ □ ^{SL}☉
④	^{SL}♆ ☌ ^{N}MC ☍ ^{SL}Asc

INNER WHEEL: Solunar Chart, Terry Schiavo, Moon Transiting 10° ♈ 57'11"
Time: March 11, 2005 (Friday), 3:40:34 p.m. EST +5:00
Location: Pinellas Park, FL, USA 27°N50'33" 082°W41'59"

OUTER WHEEL: Natal Chart, Terry Schiavo (death)
Time: March 31, 2005 (Thursday), 9:05 a.m. EST +5:00
Location: Pinellas Park, FL, USA 27°N50'33" 082°W41'59"

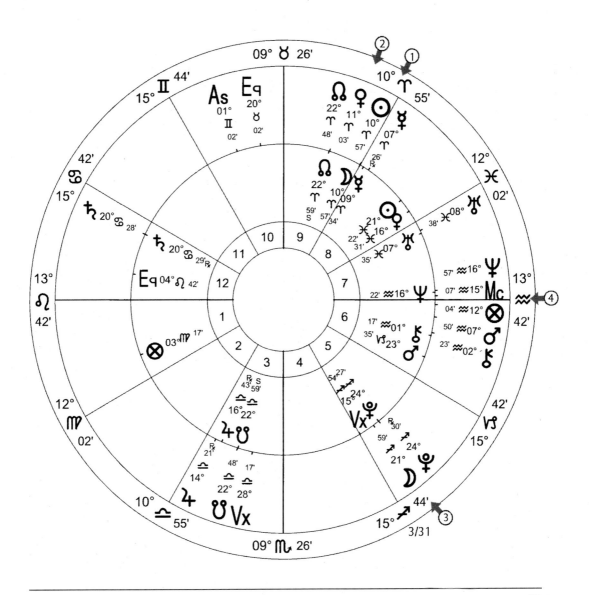

A Family Member

Especially when you are learning a new technique, it is useful to run charts on people in your family. This is an interesting chart of a member of my family that shows a separation and a new beginning.

In Pennsylvania where she was born, they did not record daylight savings time until 1971. I always wondered whether her time of birth was correct. Did the hospital use the daylight saving time, or didn't they? However when I saw this chart, I knew it was right.

But even knowing it was accurate, I didn't know what to make of it when I saw this chart. She and her husband had only been married fifteen months, but the chart seemed to indicate a coming separation. I wondered if they were going to be talking about divorce.

We have zero Virgo on her Ascendant, and natal Uranus conjuncts the solunar Midheaven. I saw that zero again. Her natal Moon at 7° Aquarius on the midpoint of Mercury/Neptune. And look at her natal Ascendant on the 4th house cusp.

As the transiting Moon on March 19 was at 28° Taurus conjunct the Midheaven, we got word that her husband had suddenly passed away. Zero degrees. It was time for her to start a new life. When you rectify a chart you can come within minutes. Notice the intercepted 10th and 4th houses.

While this was a terrible time for her, she has since started a new life and has a wonderful new husband.

The following notes refer to the numbered arrows on the chart:

①	ᔆᴸ☾ ☌ ᴺ☉ in the 10th house intercepted
②	Asc 0° ♍ 40'
③	ᴺAsc ☌ 4th house cusp
④	ᴺ☾ ☌ ᔆᴸ☿ and ♆ ruler of the 1st and 7th houses
⑤	ᵀ☾ March 19 = 28° ♉ ☌ MC ☌ ᴺ♅

INNER WHEEL: Natal Chart, Family Member, Moon Transiting 21° Ⅱ 28'45"
Time: February 21, 2002 (Thursday), 6:01 p.m. MST +7:00
Location: Mesa, AZ, USA 33°N25'20" 111°W49'19"

OUTER WHEEL: Natal Chart, Family Member
Time: June 12, 1941 (Thursday), 5:21 p.m. EST +5:00
Location: Philadelphia, PA, USA 39°N57'08" 075°W09'51"

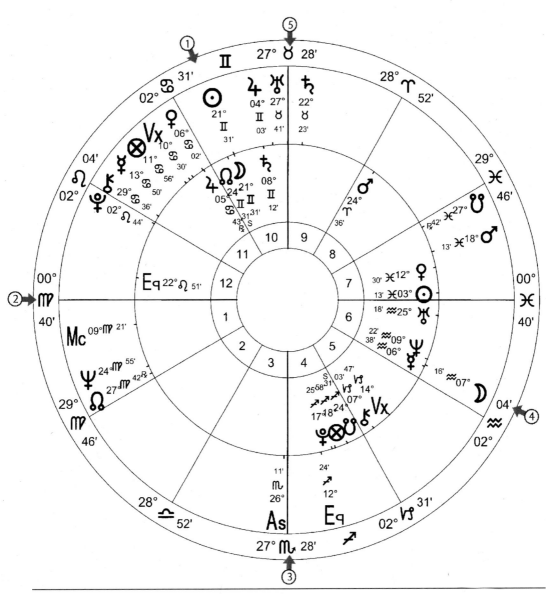

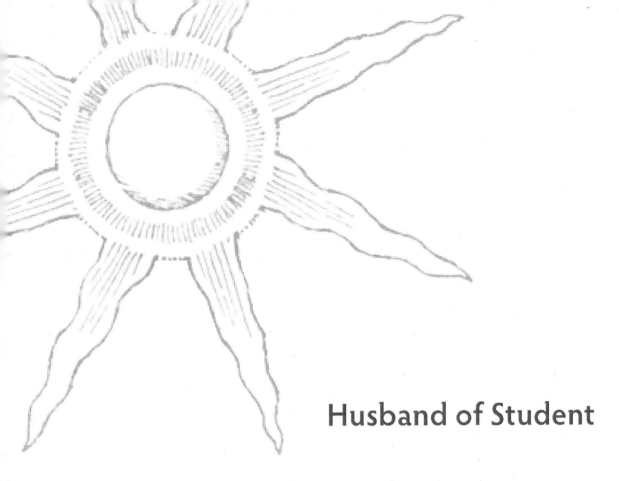

Husband of Student

Next we'll look at the chart of the husband of one of my students who winters in Arizona. When I ran her solunar chart and saw that it nearly duplicated her natal chart, I knew it would be an important month for her.

On the chart for my student's husband, the solunar took place in the 2nd house at 5° Gemini. His natal Ascendant is 2° Aries, opposite the natal vertex and solunar vertex. He was taken to the hospital unexpectedly with what turned out to be throat cancer. The Part of Surgery is 16° Libra, within 2 degrees of Jupiter. His Jupiter/Saturn midpoint is 5° Virgo.

When you have a planet in the degree of the node, a red flag should go up—and this was exactly the case with Pluto. The antiscian of the full Moon is 24° Aries conjunct the node, and the antiscian of the Sun is 1° Scorpio 56'. These points don't lie. Notice the intercepted 12th and 6th houses.

The following notes refer to the numbered arrows on the chart:

①	^{SL}☽ ☌ ^{N}☉ in the 2nd house ☌ the 3rd house cusp
②	♃/♄ 5° ♍ in the 6th house □ ^{SL}☽ 5° ♊ (OOB) ☍ ^{SL}♅ in the 12th house
③	Full ☽ February 23 = 5° ♍ on ♃/♄ midpoint
④	^{SL}Vx ☌ ^{N}Vx on the 7th house cusp
⑤	Part of Surgery, Asc + ♄-♂ =16° ♎ 06' ☌ ^{SL}♃
⑥	Antiscia of ^{SL}☉ 1° ♏ 56' ☌ ^{N}☊
⑦	^{N}Asc 2° ♈ 43' ☌ ^{SL}Asc 1° ♈ 40' ☍ Vx
⑧	^{N}♂ (ruler of Asc) ☌ ^{SL}☊ in same degree as ^{SL}♀ Antiscia of Full ☽ 25°♈ ☌ ^{N}♂ and ^{SL}☊
	^{SL}☽ + 24°27' and ♂- 23°40' (OOB) ruling angles

INNER WHEEL: Solunar Chart, Husband of Student, Moon Transiting 05° ♊ 18'25"
Time: February 16, 2005 (Wednesday), 8:44:44 a.m. MST +7:00
Location: Mesa, AZ, USA 33°N25'20" 111°W49'19"

OUTER WHEEL: Natal Chart, Husband of Student
Time: May 27, 1930 (Tuesday), 2:15 a.m. CDT +6:00
Location: Crookston, MN, USA 47°N46'27" 096°W36'28"

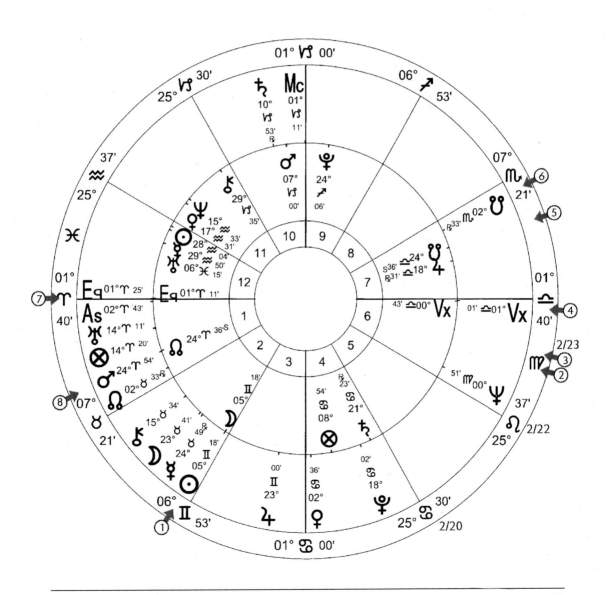

Daughter and Granddaughter

We are all interconnected, affecting the people around us, and you can see that when you look at the charts. I'll present several charts to show the connection between myself, my daughter, and my granddaughter.

This is my chart in 1979. With my natal 8th house coming to the solunar Ascendant, my solunar falling in the 5th house of children conjunct Venus, I was expecting something having to do with money or my kids. So how bad could it be? Will my kid come calling to ask for money?

It turned out that my daughter did call me, but it was to tell me that she was getting married—she didn't need any money and she wasn't pregnant, thanks be to God. But her natal Venus of 10° Virgo was on the solunar node and Saturn, ruler of the Ascendant. So I knew there was something more going on.

They were married June 29. A new Moon fell on the solunar Sun at 2° Cancer, so I became suspicious. I couldn't help wondering what would happen. Notice the intercepted 2nd and 8th houses.

The following notes refer to the numbered arrows on the chart:

①	^{SL}☽ ♂ ^{N}☉ in the 5th house
②	New ☽ 2° ♋ ♂ ^{SL}☉
③	Daughter's ^{N}♀= 10° ♍ ♂ ^{SL}♄ and ☊ ruler of the Asc

INNER WHEEL: Solunar Chart, Daughter, Moon Transiting 14° Ⅱ 26'19"
Time: June 22, 1979 (Friday), 10:04:16 p.m. EDT +4:00
Location: Verona, NJ, USA 40°N49'47" 074°W14'26"

OUTER WHEEL: Natal Chart, Anne Vick
Time: June 5, 1924 (Thursday), 5:57 a.m. EDT +4:00
Location: Newark, NJ, USA 40°N44'08" 074°W10'22"

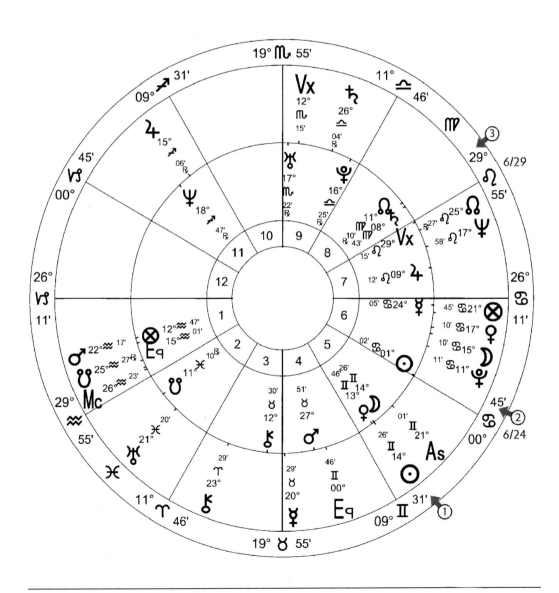

Next is the solunar chart for their wedding. There's a lot going on in this chart. The natal Ascendant is trine the solunar Ascendant. The 0° Taurus on the Midheaven indicates a new beginning. Other interesting things in this chart are natal Mars on solunar Mercury and Sun, natal Mercury on solunar Jupiter, natal Jupiter on solunar Ascendant at 12° Leo, natal Moon on solunar Saturn.

The following notes refer to the numbered arrows on the chart:

①	^{SL}☽ ☌ ^{N}☉ in the 11th house of hopes and desires
②	^{N}☿ ☌ ^{SL}♃
③	^{N}♃ ☌ ^{SL}Asc
④	^{SL}Asc △ ^{N}Asc
⑤	^{N}☽ ☌ ^{SL}♄
⑥	^{N}☊ ☌ ^{SL}Part of Fortune, △ ^{SL}♀, ☋ and ♂ in the 10th house
⑦	^{SL}MC 0° ♉ = new beginning
⑧	^{N}♂ ☌ ^{SL}☿ and ☉ in the 10th house

INNER WHEEL: Solunar Chart, Wedding, Moon Transiting 07° ♎ 33'37"
Time: May 28, 1979 (Monday), 10:15:14 a.m. EDT +4:00
Location: Brighton, MA, USA 42°N21' 071°W09'25"

OUTER WHEEL: Natal Chart, Wedding
Time: June 29, 1979 (Friday), 6:07 p.m. EDT +4:00
Location: Brighton, MA, USA 42°N21' 071°W09'25"

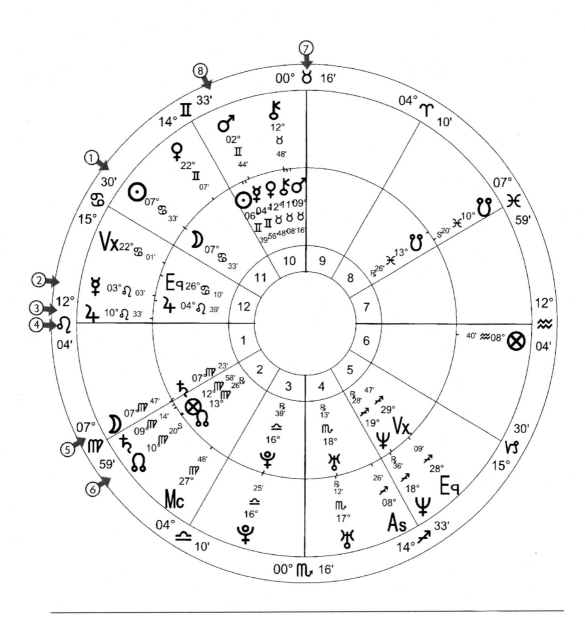

Next is the solunar return before the birth of my daughter's child, my granddaughter.

With Jupiter in the 12th house, my daughter was taken to the hospital three weeks before my granddaughter was born with the threat of a miscarriage. Notice all the 7s in the charts: Uranus at 7°, Jupiter at 7° (wedding), and the Sun and Moon also 7° and inconjunct each other in the houses of health (Jupiter and Uranus square Moon, inconjunct the Sun). Notice the intercepted 3rd and 9th houses.

Everything turned out alright, but it was a serious matter that nearly ended very badly.

The following notes refer to the numbered arrows on the chart:

①	^{SL}☽ ☌ ^{N}☉ in the 7th house
②	Part of Marriage 24° ♏ 45' ☍ ^{SL}☉
③	^{SL}♃ and ♅ ☐ ^{N}☽ intercepted, ⚻ ^{N}☉
④	^{N}Asc ☌ ♃ and ♅, ☐ ^{N}☽, ⚻ ^{SL}☽ and ♀
⑤	^{N}♀ ☌ ^{SL}☊ in the 7th house

INNER WHEEL: Solunar Chart, Wedding, Moon Transiting 07° ♋ 33'37"
Time: May 15, 1983 (Sunday), 9:27:31 p.m. EDT +4:00
Location: Brighton, MA, USA 42°N21' 071°W09'25"

OUTER WHEEL: Natal Chart, Daughter's Wedding
Time: June 29, 1979 (Friday), 6:07 p.m. EDT +4:00
Location: Brighton, MA, USA 42°N21' 071°W09'25"

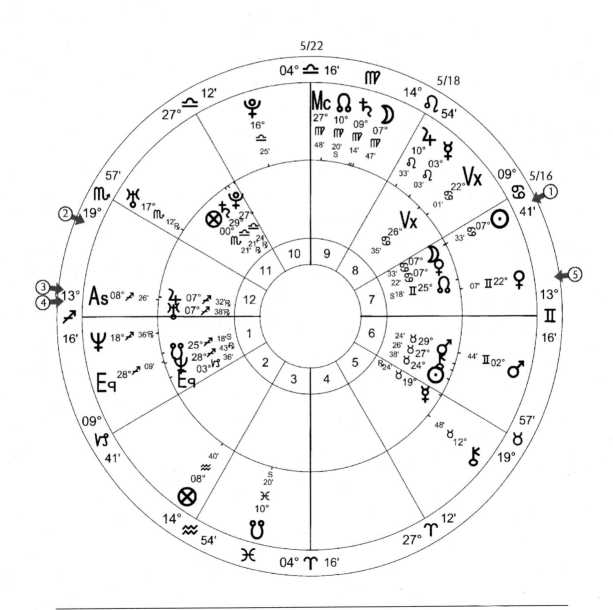

Then I wondered if I can use an event chart to see other events. In the event chart, I use the wedding as the event and put my granddaughter's natal chart on the outer wheel.

Notice the natal Moon is at 27° Virgo on the Midheaven of the wedding chart on the inner wheel. Her Ascendant is at 9° Virgo 49' on the wedding chart conjunct Saturn, the node, and the Moon.

My granddaughter was born May 21, 1983 exactly as the transiting Moon came over the natal Midheaven of the chart.

The following notes refer to the numbered arrows on the chart:

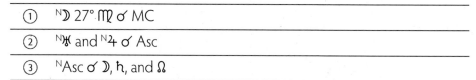

①	^{N}☽ 27° ♍ ☌ MC
②	^{N}♅ and ^{N}♃ ☌ Asc
③	^{N}Asc ☌ ☽, ♄, and ☊

INNER WHEEL: Natal Chart, Daughter's Wedding
Time: June 29, 1979 (Friday), 6:07 p.m. EDT +4:00
Location: Brighton, MA, USA 42°N21' 071°W09'25"

OUTER WHEEL: Natal Chart, Birth of Child
Time: May 21, 1983 (Saturday), 1:06 p.m. EDT +4:00
Location: Brighton, MA, USA 42°N21' 071°W09'25"

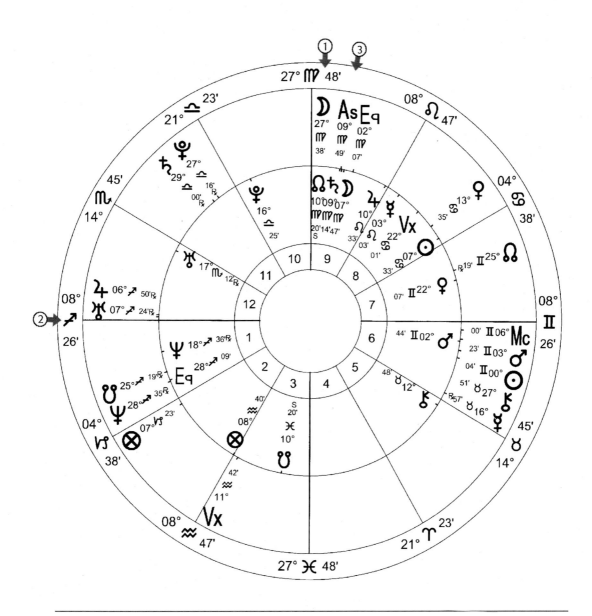

Anne N. Vick

A great way to experiment with a new technique is to run charts on yourself. I will present several charts on myself here for you.

In 1981 I was washing the ceiling in my kitchen (who washes ceilings?) and I fell. Mercury, the ruler of my Sun, is on the solunar 4th house cusp and was retrograde. Because Mercury is the ruler of my chart, the best way for me to work it out is physically.

This is a reactive chart, because most of the planets are over on the Libra side of the chart. So I was reacting – and let me tell you, I was in a cast all the way down, I could do nothing for myself, so I had to depend on everybody. This went on for four months.

When you get a ruler of an angle on an angle, this is something to take very seriously. In my case, solunar Venus was in the 7th house and ruler the 4th. My natal 6th house cusp is 21° Scorpio on the natal 10th house; and there was a lunar eclipse at 24° Capricorn, close to the Ascendant on the chart. My natal Midheaven is 26° Aquarius squaring solunar Uranus, the ruler of an angle on an angle.

Sixteen days later, on July 15, I fell and ended up in a wheelchair for four months. So if I would progress the solunar Midheaven one degree per day for sixteen days, that would be 7°, almost 8° Sagittarius, which is inconjunct the solunar Sun in the 6th house.

Look where Chiron is, on my 4th house cusp. My fall could have been much more serious: if I'd fallen in a different direction I could have been killed. When I landed, I couldn't reach the phone, but luckily my son called for me. Over the radio I heard "Some old lady has fallen." I told my son to call them and set them straight! I'm not some old lady. *Now* I'm an old lady, but not back in 1981!

Now whenever I see my natal Saturn square the solunar Ascendant, I know I'm in trouble right away. Notice the intercepted 1st and 7th houses.

The following notes refer to the numbered arrows on the chart:

①	^{SL}☽ ☌ ^{N}☉ in the 5th house
②	^{SL}♀ on 7th house cusp, ruler of the 4th and 9th houses ☌ ^{SL}♌
③	^{N}6th house cusp 21° ♏ ☌ ^{SL}MC
④	$^{P\,SL}$MC 8° ♐ ⊼ ^{SL}☉ in the 6th house
⑤	Lunar Eclipse 24° ♑ ☌ ^{SL}Asc
⑥	^{N}MC 26° ♒ □ ^{SL}♅ and □ ^{SL}MC

INNER WHEEL: Solunar Chart, Anne Vick, Moon Transiting 14° Ⅱ 26'19"
Time: June 29, 1981 (Monday), 9:41:48 p.m. EDT +4:00
Location: Verona, NJ, USA 40°N49'47" 074°W14'26"

OUTER WHEEL: Natal Chart, Anne Vick
Time: June 5, 1924 (Thursday), 5:57 a.m. EDT +4:00
Location: Newark, NJ, USA 40°N44'08" 074°W10'22"

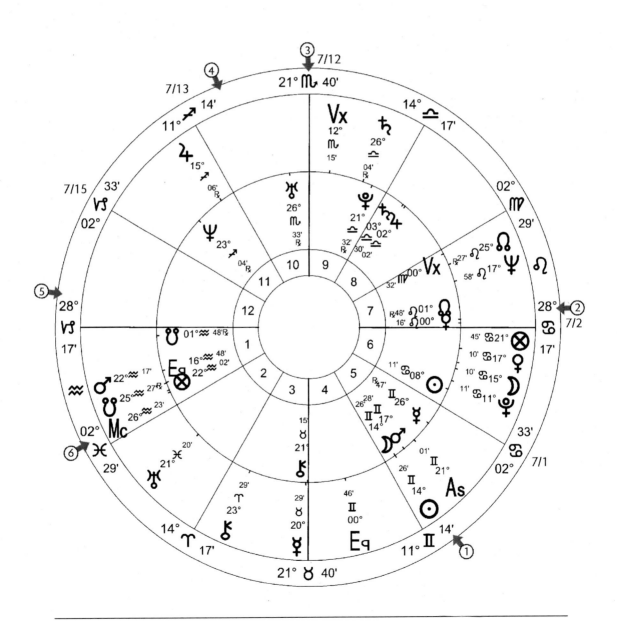

Now we're getting more current. Let's talk more about timing on a chart. The following chart is from January 31, 2004. My solunar is in the 8th house – the house of surgeries among other things. Venus, which is the ruler of the Ascendant, is square to Pluto.

Remember one of the rules: when the transiting Moon comes to conjunct the ruler of the Ascendant, we know we've got a problem there already. The new Moon on February 20 was at 1° Pisces. My progressed Sun was 0° Virgo. When that Moon came to February 21, I was taken to the hospital, an emergency. On the 25th, when the Moon got to Mars, I had surgery – and that one was right on. The square makes you wonder right away what was going on. My progressed Mars was at 0° Pisces, but my natal Uranus is 21° Pisces right on the Venus. Talk about timing!

The following notes refer to the numbered arrows on the chart:

①	^{SL}☽ ♂ ^{N}☉ in the 8th house
②	^{P}☉ (from progressed chart, not shown) 0° ♍ 39' ☍ New ☽ at 1° ♓ ♂ ^{SL}♅
③	^{N}♄ ♂ ^{SL}Asc □ MC
④	^{N}♃ ☍ ^{SL}☽ □ ^{SL}♃
⑤	Lunar Eclipse 24° ♑ ♂ 4th house
⑥	^{SL}♀ ♂ ^{N}♅ □ ^{SL}♀ (♀ ruler of the Asc and 8th house)
⑦	Surgery on February 25 ♂ ^{SL}♂ on the 7th house cusp

INNER WHEEL: Solunar Chart, Anne Vick, Moon Transiting 14° Ⅱ 26'19"
Time: January 31, 2004 (Saturday), 11:40:55 p.m. MST +7:00
Location: Mesa, AZ, USA 33°N25'20" 111°W49'19"

OUTER WHEEL: Natal Chart, Anne Vick
Time: June 5, 1924 (Thursday), 5:57 a.m. EDT +4:00
Location: Newark, NJ, USA 40°N44'08" 074°W10'22"

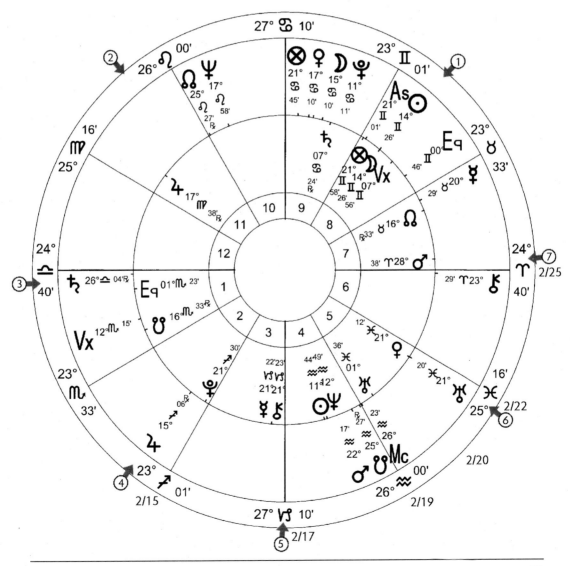

I have one more personal chart to share which is a good example of the effect of vertex. I seem to get a lot of 8th house stuff! Notice my natal vertex is exactly on my 10th house cusp, and my solunar falls in my 5th house, again, children. The ruler of the solunar Ascendant is Saturn, and Saturn is in the 5th house. Solunar Neptune is square the Midheaven and vertex. The natal node is 25° Leo, opposing solunar Uranus. When the solunar Moon came around to the Saturn, that was the day my son passed away. Notice the intercepted 2nd and 8th houses.

The following notes refer to the numbered arrows on the chart:

①	ˢᴸ☽ ♂ ᴺ☉ in the 5th house
②	☽/☉ midpoint 29° ♊ 48' ♂ ˢᴸ♃, △ ˢᴸ☉
③	ᴺ♀ OOB ruler of the 4th and 9th houses
④	ᴺ☊ ♂ ˢᴸVx ☍ ˢᴸ♅ and ᴺMC
⑤	ᴺVx ♂ the 10th house cusp
⑥	♂/♄ midpoint 24° ♐ 11' ♂ ˢᴸ☋
⑦	ᴺ8th house on ˢᴸ1st house
⑧	ˢᴸ♆ □ ᴺVx and ˢᴸMC
⑨	ˢᴸ♅ ☍ Vx ♂ ᴺMC ♂ ᴺ☋ and ♂
⑩	Asc/MC midpoint 23° ♈ 42' ♂ ᴺ⚷, ˢᴸ♂ co-ruler of the 10th house

Part of Sons: 20° ♏ 58' ☍ ᴺ☿
Part of Daughters: 23° ♊ 02' ♂ ᴺAsc and ˢᴸ☊
Part of Death: 20° ♐ 32' ♂ ♂/♄ midpoint

Note from the editor:

There actually are a few more charts about Anne in this book. With her strong focus on teaching others about solunar charts, I'm sure she would never forgive us if we neglected to include the solunar charts showing her death—as she passed from this world so close to the time of her solunar return. Please refer to the chapter "Anne's Final Solunar Return" on page 101.

INNER WHEEL: Solunar Chart, Anne Vick, Moon Transiting 14° Ⅱ 26'19"
Time: February 21, 2002 (Thursday), 5:01:13 a.m. MST +7:00
Location: Mesa, AZ, USA 33°N25'20" 111°W49'19"

OUTER WHEEL: Natal Chart, Anne Vick
Time: June 5, 1924 (Thursday), 5:57 a.m. EDT +4:00
Location: Newark, NJ, USA 40°N44'08" 074°W10'22"

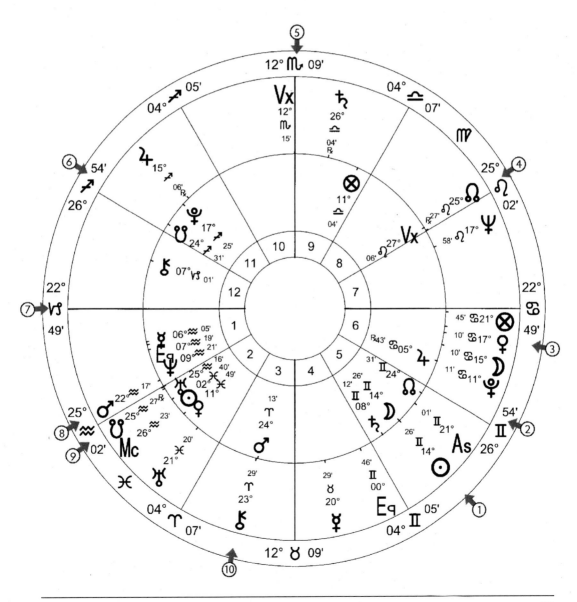

Enrose House

Sometimes it can be interesting to run a chart on a house or other building. You might want to run a chart on your house to choose times for placing it on the market, begin renovations, use it as the place for an event, or anything else you want to do with the house. There are several ways you can run the chart, but a good way is to use the official recording time of the deed.

When I looked at the natal chart for our house, I saw that the Ascendant and transiting Uranus was around 7° Aquarius. I said to my husband, "Is this house going to blow up?" I ran a solunar chart to see what's happening. Below is the deed chart for our house at 5245 E. Enrose.

The solunar Moon is in the 4th house, and the natal vertex is on the 4th house cusp. The natal node conjuncts the solunar Mars and Jupiter in the 9th house. The solunar Ascendant is the same as Anne's natal Ascendant, so I thought this was an important time. Natal Pluto conjuncts the solunar vertex. Natal Uranus and Saturn conjunct solunar Mercury, ruler of the Ascendant and the 4th house. The natal Moon is at 28° Scorpio, square the solunar Midheaven. I was a little bit fearful when I saw solunar Uranus with my natal Ascendant. This was very unsettling, so on January 24 my husband and I decided that we needed to give the house a new natal chart. We took it from a jointly-owned home to a home owned in a trust—changing the deed and the natal chart.

The following notes refer to the numbered arrows on the chart:

①	^{SL}☽ ☌ ^{N}☉ in the 4th house
②	^{N}♀ ☌ ^{SL}Vx
③	^{N}♅ and ♄ ☌ ^{SL}☿ ruler of the Asc and 4th house
④	^{SL}♅ ☌ ^{N}Asc
⑤	^{N}☊ ☌ ^{SL}♂ and ♃ in the 9th house
⑥	^{SL}Asc same as Anne's natal Asc (Anne's natal chart not shown)
⑦	^{N}Vx ☌ 4th house cusp

INNER WHEEL: Solunar Chart, House Deed, Moon Transiting 14° ♍ 21'13"
Time: January 16, 1998 (Friday), 3:05:56 p.m. MST +7:00
Location: Phoenix, AZ, USA 33°N26'54" 112°W04'24"

OUTER WHEEL: Natal Chart, House Deed
Time: September 6, 1989 (Wednesday), 4:55 p.m. MST +7:00
Location: Phoenix, AZ, USA 33°N26'54" 112°W04'24"

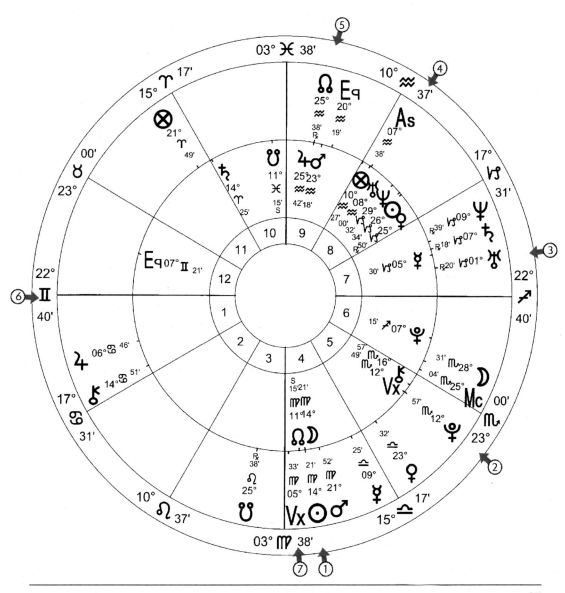

Solunar Chart Workshop: Michael Jackson's Death

Michael Jackson died after Anne, or else she would have included a solunar chart showing his death. In this chapter we will use Anne's rules to view the death event for each of the two birth times that we have for Michael Jackson.

Now that you have read Anne's book, let's approach these charts as a test or a workshop. I will show the charts and list some of the pertinent information you should use for interpretation, based on the list in "Interpreting the solunar chart" on page 7. See if you can find the correct locations and mark them on the charts.

First we will look at the chart of his death, for which of course we have the accurate time. Following that we will look at charts using the natal time from Dietrech Pessin (the charts labeled #1) and from Virginia Reyer (the charts labeled #2).

We will start with the chart showing the death. Michael Jackson died June 25, 2009 12:21 p.m. in Los Angeles.

The following notes refer to the chart. Place letters around the chart to show their proper positions:

Ⓐ	Solar eclipse on January 25, 2009, Los Angeles, California at 11:55 pm PST. These are the important points of the eclipse: MC 4° ♌, Asc 0° ♏, ☽ and ☉ 6° ♒ 29, Vx 15° ♊ 43'
Ⓑ	Summer Solstice, June 20
Ⓒ	New Moon June 22 at 1° ♋ 30' ☍ ♀ (in 4th house, same wheel as his death chart). The Moon by longitude is too wide for a ☍ to ♆ and ♃, but by declination is contraparallel (☽ +14°31' ♆ -13°08' ♃ -13°25') and should be considered.
Ⓓ	What houses are the planets in and where do they rule?
Ⓔ	Michael's prenatal solar eclipse is 28°♈ 34' ⊼ the Asc of the death chart.
Ⓕ	Midpoints: ☽/☉ 25° ♋ 23', Asc/MC 11° ♌ 32', ♂/♄ 17° ♋ 17', ♂/♅ 22° ♈ 28'
Ⓖ	Part of Death: 6° ♊ 53'
Ⓗ	Antiscia: ☉ 25° ♊ 38' ♂ MC, MC 3° ♋ 36' ♂ ☉, ☽ 13° ♉ 35' ♂ ♂ and ♀, Asc 3° ♈ 18' □ ♀ □ ☉

Natal Chart, Michael Jackson (death)
Time: June 25, 2009 (Thursday), 12:21 p.m. PDT +7:00
Location: Los Angeles, CA, USA 34°N03'08" 118°W14'34"

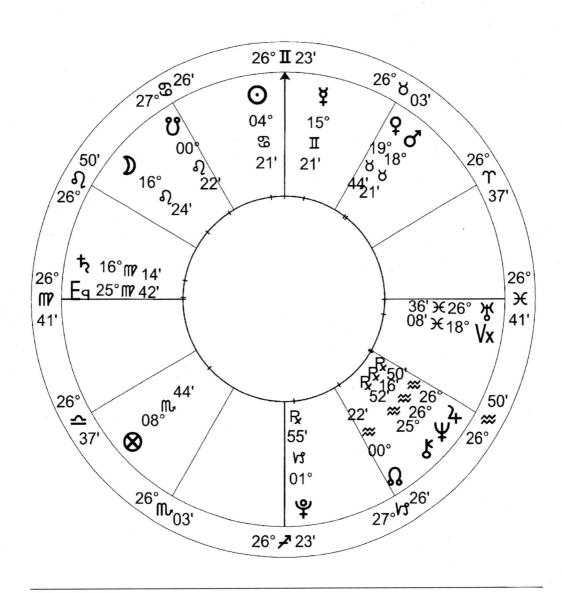

Let's look at the secondary progressed charts. This first chart uses the time from Dietrech Pessin.

The following notes refer to the chart. Place letters around the chart to show their proper positions:

Ⓐ	Michael's prenatal solar eclipse is 28° ♈ 34' ☌ ☋ □ ^{P}☽, ☍ ^{P}☉
Ⓑ	^{P}Asc: □ ♇, □ ^{N}☉, ☍ ^{P}♂ ℞
Ⓒ	^{P}☽: □ ^{P}☉, □ ☊ ☋, □ ^{N}♃, ⚻ ^{N}Vx
Ⓓ	^{P}♅: ☌ ^{N}♀, ☍ ⚷, □ ^{N}♂, □ ^{P}Asc
Ⓔ	^{P}Vx □ ^{P}♀ and ☊ ☋, ☍ ^{P}☽
Ⓕ	**Midpoints**: ☽/☉ 10° ♐ 20', Asc/MC 23° ♎ 31', ♂/♄ 11° ♓ 43' ☌ ^{N}☽ in 4th house
Ⓖ	Part of Death: 7° ♉ 37' Part of Danger: 16° ♎ 17' Part of Fatality: 28° ♑ 41' ☌ ☽, □ prenatal eclipse
Ⓗ	**Antiscia**: Asc 27° ♑ 13', MC 15° ♈ 43', ☉ 4° ♓ 21', ☽ 4° ♐ 57', ☊ 7° ♓/♍ 43', ♂ 28° ♋ 05' ℞, ♀ 10° ♓ 12'

INNER WHEEL: Natal Chart, Michael Jackson (#1)
Time: August 29, 1958 (Friday), 12:09 p.m. CDT +5:00
Location: Gary, IN, USA 41°N35'36" 087°W20'47"

OUTER WHEEL: Secondary Progressed Chart, Michael Jackson (death)
Time: June 25, 2009 (Thursday), 12:21 p.m. PDT +7:00
Location: Los Angeles, CA, USA 34°N03'08" 118°W14'34"

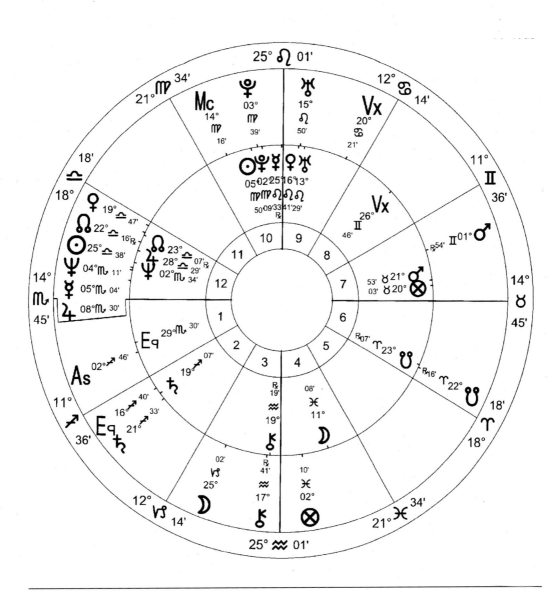

Here is the secondary progressed chart using the time from Virginia Reyer.

The following notes refer to the chart. Place letters around the chart to show their proper positions:

Ⓐ	Michael's prenatal solar eclipse is 28° ♈ 34' ☌ ☋, ☍ N♃ and P☉
Ⓑ	PAsc: 29° ♊ 31' (at the A point with ♅, sudden event affecting the world) □ ♀
Ⓒ	P☽: 1° ♒ 22' ⚻ ♀, △ P♂ ℞ (ruling Asc and intercepted 4th)
Ⓓ	P♅: 16° ♌ ☌ ♀ ☍ MC
Ⓔ	PMC: ⚼ P☉, ☍ N☉,
Ⓕ	P♃ ☌ NVx
Ⓖ	Midpoints: ☽/☉ 13° ♐ 45', Asc/MC 5° ♉ 15', ♂/♄ 11° ♓ 43'
Ⓗ	Part of Death: 22° ♊ 16' Part of Danger: 29° ♊ 31' Part of Fatality: 24° ♌ 59'
Ⓘ	Antiscia: Asc 0° ♋ 28', MC 19° ♎ 01', ☉ 3° ♓ 52', ☽ 28° ♏ 37', ☊ 7° ♓/♍ 43', ♂ 28° ♋ 09' ℞, ♀ 9° ♓ 35'

INNER WHEEL: Natal Chart, Michael Jackson (#2)
Time: August 29, 1958 (Friday), 11:53 p.m. CDT +5:00
Location: Gary, IN, USA 41°N35'36" 087°W20'47"

OUTER WHEEL: Secondary Progressed Chart, Michael Jackson (death)
Time: June 25, 2009 (Thursday), 12:21 p.m. PDT +7:00
Location: Los Angeles, CA, USA 34°N03'08" 118°W14'34"

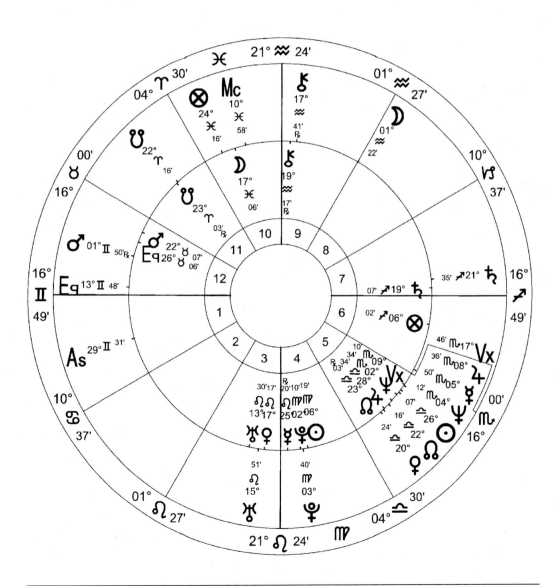

Now let's look at the solunar return charts for the time of death, starting with the chart using the time from Dietrech Pessin.

The following notes refer to the chart. Place letters around the chart to show their proper positions:

Ⓐ	Michael's prenatal solar eclipse is 28° ♈ 34' ♂ ♀, ♂ ♂, ☍ ♃, △ MC and ☿
Ⓑ	Put the transiting Moon around the chart: June 4 at 11° ♏, June 11 at 5° ♒, June 18 at 3° ♉, June 25 at 16° ♌
Ⓒ	Solunar in 12th house
Ⓓ	♅ □ ᴺVx
Ⓔ	♆, ♃, and ☋ ☍ ᴺMC and ☿
Ⓕ	☊ □ ᴺ♆
Ⓖ	♀ ♂ ᴺ☋, △ MC and ☿
Ⓗ	♂ ☍ ᴺ♃
Ⓘ	MC ☍ ᴺ♄
Ⓙ	☿ ♉ Vx -15°02
Ⓚ	♆ turned retrograde May 29 at 26° ♒ 29'
Ⓛ	♀ turned direct May 31 at 22° ♉ 53'
Ⓜ	♃ turned retrograde June 15 at 27° ♒ 01'
Ⓝ	Declination: ☿ +14°57' ruling Asc and MC ♉ Vx -15°02'

INNER WHEEL: Solunar Chart, Michael Jackson, Moon Transiting 05° ♍ 50'44"
Time: May 30, 2009 (Saturday), 1:25:02 p.m. PDT +7:00
Location: Santa Maria, CA, USA 34°N57'11" 120°W26'05"

OUTER WHEEL: Natal Chart, Michael Jackson (#1)
Time: August 29, 1958 (Friday), 12:09 p.m. CDT +5:00
Location: Gary, IN, USA 41°N35'36" 087°W20'47"

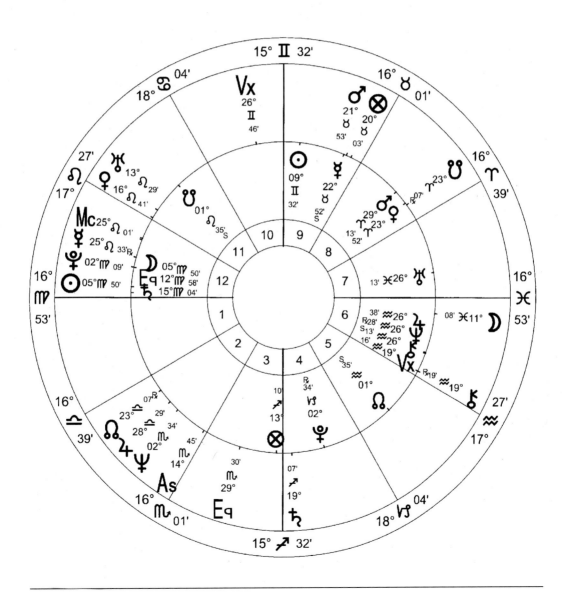

Here is the solunar return chart using the time from Virginia Reyer.

The following notes refer to the chart. Place letters around the chart to show their proper positions:

Ⓐ	Michael's prenatal solar eclipse is 28° ♈ 34' ♂ 8th house cusp and ♂, ⊼ Asc
Ⓑ	Put the transiting Moon around the chart: June 4 at 11° ♏, June 11 at 5° ♒, June 18 at 3° ♉, June 25 at 16° ♌
Ⓒ	Solunar in 12th house ♂ ♀
Ⓓ	♅ ♂ 7th house, ☍ Asc
Ⓔ	♀ ⊼ ☋
Ⓕ	♌ ⊼ ᴺ♀, ᴺ☉
Ⓖ	♆, ♃, and ☋ ♂ ᴺMC, ☍ ᴺ☿
Ⓗ	♀ ♂ ᴺ☋
Ⓘ	☿ ♂ ᴺ♂
Ⓙ	♄ ☐ ᴺAsc, ☐ ᴺ♄
Ⓚ	Vx ♂ ᴺ☽
Ⓛ	♆ turned retrograde May 29 at 6° ♒ 29'
Ⓜ	☿ turned direct May 31 at 22° ♉ 53'
Ⓝ	♃ turned retrograde June 15 at 27° ♒ 01'

INNER WHEEL: Solunar Chart, Michael Jackson, Moon Transiting 06° ♍ 19'04"
Time: May 30, 2009 (Saturday), 2:14:22 p.m. PDT +7:00
Location: Santa Maria, CA, USA 34°N57'11" 120°W26'05"

OUTER WHEEL: Natal Chart, Michael Jackson (#2)
Time: August 29, 1958 (Friday), 11:53 p.m. CDT +5:00
Location: Gary, IN, USA 41°N35'36" 087°W20'47"

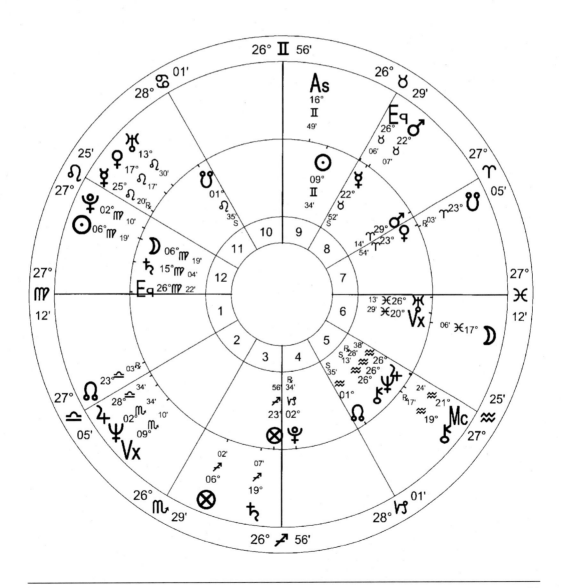

Anne's Final Solunar Return

As Dietrech Pessin said in her forward to this book, Anne seemed to have called out to make her most poignant case for the value of solunar returns when she passed away within hours of her final solunar on December 12, 2008.

Ever interested in promoting the knowledge and use of solunar returns as an important tool for timing, we're sure Anne would have wanted us to use the charts of her own passing as yet another example of this tool in use.

The solunar return is shown on page 102 and the progressed chart is on page 103. We'll discuss the charts on the pages following.

INNER WHEEL: Solunar Chart, Anne Vick, Moon Transiting 14° Ⅱ 26'19"
Time: December 11, 2008 (Thursday), 11:17:20 p.m. MST +7:00
Location: Mesa, AZ, USA 33°N25'20" 111°W49'19"

OUTER WHEEL: Natal Chart, Anne Vick
Time: June 5, 1924 (Thursday), 5:57 a.m. EDT +4:00
Location: Newark, NJ, USA 40°N44'08" 074°W10'22"

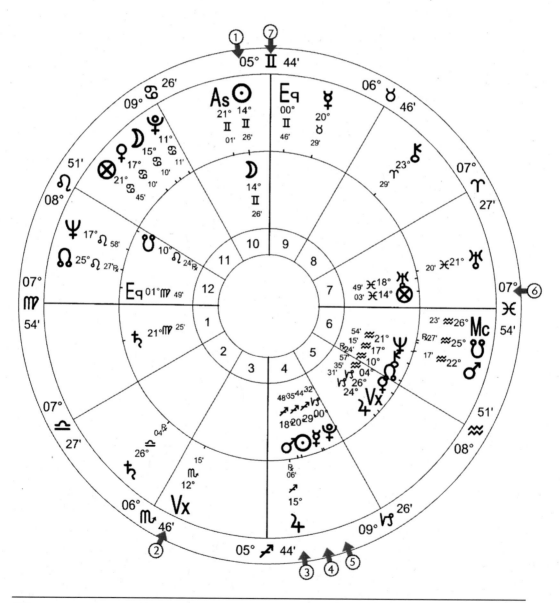

INNER WHEEL: Natal Chart, Anne Vick
Time: June 5, 1924 (Thursday), 5:57 a.m. EDT +4:00
Location: Newark, NJ, USA 40°N44'08" 074°W10'22"

OUTER WHEEL: Progressed Chart, Anne Vick
Time: December 12, 2008 (Friday), 9:06 a.m. MST +7:00
Location: Mesa, AZ, USA 33°N25'20" 111°W49'19"

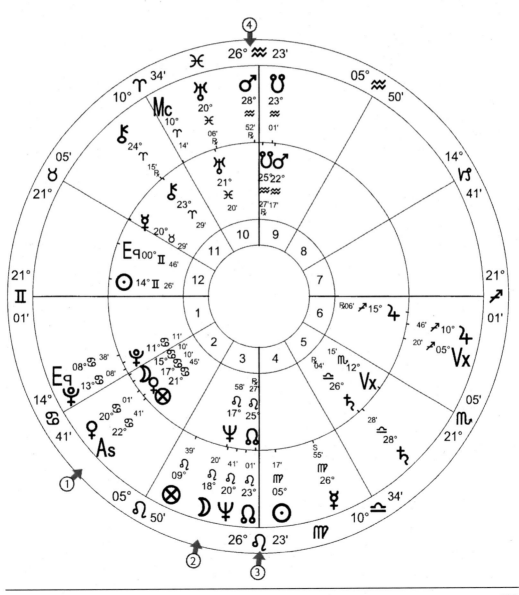

As I look at Anne's charts my heart is very sad to have lost a dear friend and colleague. Than I have to realize how lucky I was to have know and studied with her. I must remember that we choose our chart. Thank you Anne for all you gave, physically, mentally, emotionally, and spiritually.

First I see the Solunar in the 10th house of reputations and success. She must have known that she had finished what she came to do, leaving the rest for us to work on. She wrote so much on the Vertex and we can see evidence of this in her two charts.

I was taught years ago: "the 8th house is how you die, but you leave this planet through the 4th house." I have not done the full research on this, but what I have seen so far seems to support it. Also I was taught that you are tied to the earth on the Cross of Matter, which is your angles in the chart.

Anne's natal 8th house is in Capricorn ruled by Saturn, showing a possible long or difficult illness—and she did have a long illness. Her Saturn is trine the Midheaven, which reflects the positive attitude that Anne had during this time.

Her natal 4th house is in Leo ruled by the Sun, where you shine. Her Sun was in the 12th house of knowing and the unknown, so she could see behind the curtain. Her 4th house is involved in all the charts. When you look at the Solunar chart you see Sagittarius on the 4th house cusp with natal Jupiter there also, and so strong in its own sign. When Jupiter was activated, it give her the opportunity to take a long trip, even if metaphorically.

Another old astrology rule is: for a major event to occur you need at least three hits to the charts for it to manifest. In Anne's charts we have the following aspects:

- Progressed Nodal return in the 9th house conjunct natal Mars inconjunct the progressed Ascendant

- Progressed Sun 05° Virgo 17' conjunct the solunar Ascendant, square the angles

- Progressed Vertex inconjunct 05° Sagittarius 20' conjunct the solunar 4th house cusp

- Progressed Part of Death 22° Capricorn 39' conjunct the solunar Jupiter and the Vertex

- Progressed Mars/Saturn midpoint is at 28° Sagittarius 40' conjunct the solunar Mercury and Pluto in the 4th house

- Progressed Moon/Sun midpoint is at 26° Leo 49' conjunct the natal 4th house cusp and Nodes

- Natal Sun conjunct Solunar Moon opposite Jupiter and Mars in the 4th house

- Solunar Mars/Saturn midpoint is at 5° Scorpio 06' inconjunct the solunar Midheaven, square the solunar Venus

The Prenatal Solar eclipse shows what you need to do to help others. Anne's prenatal was 14° Pisces 49', square her natal Sun. This reveals that her sensitivities, understanding, and ability to feel her own and others' pain was developed and she needed to teach others this awareness. This was brought to her attention by her solunar Moon/Sun midpoint being here. Again, as this squared the Solunar chart her conscious and unconscious was stirred.

Finally, in the solunar chart, her Moon is out of bounds (OOB) +26°44' ruling the 11th house. Her Mercury was OOB -25°25' ruling the Ascendant and Midheaven. Her Mars was OOB -23°29' ruling the 3rd and 8th houses. With these planets out of bounds, the rules were broken—need we say more?

The following notes refer to the numbered arrows on the solunar chart:

①	^{SL}☽ ☌ ^{N}☉ in the 10th house
②	^{N}Vx ⊼ ^{SL}☽ in the 10th house
③	^{N}♃ in its own sign ♐ (in 4th house) ☌ ^{SL}♂ (ruler of 8th house) and ☌ ^{SL}☉, ☍ ^{SL}☽ and ^{N}☉ in the 10th house
④	^{SL}"T" square ☉, ♄, and ♅, with ^{N}Asc in the 10th house making it a Grand Square.
⑤	^{SL}☿ at 29° (ruler of Asc and MC) ☌ ♀ in 4th house
⑥	Prenatal solar eclipse at 14° ♓ 49' in the 7th house ☌ Part of Fortune and ♅, □ ^{SL}☽ and ^{N}☉
⑦	^{SL}Mc in the sign of ♊, same as her ^{N}Asc and ☉

In the solunar chart ☽, ☿, and ♂ are OOB

☽/☉ midpoint 17° ♓ 31', Asc/MC midpoint 21° ♋ 49'

Part of Death 20° ♐ 32' ☌ ^{SL}☉ ☍ ^{N}Asc

The following notes refer to the numbered arrows on the progressed chart:

①	^{P}Asc 22° ♋ 41' ☌ ^{N}♀ and Part of Fortune
②	^{P}☽ 18° ♌ 20' ☌ ♆ ☍ ♂
③	^{P}☽/☉ midpoint 26° ♌ 49' ☌ ^{N}4th house cusp and ☊
④	^{P}♂ ☌ ^{N}MC

In the Solunar Chart:

^{P}☉ 05° ♍ 17' ☌ ^{SL}Asc

^{P}Vx 05° ♐ 20' ☌ ^{SL}4th house cusp

^{P}Part of Death 22° ♑ 39' ☌ ^{SL}♃ and Vx

Closing Notes

As you have seen, solunar charts can be a helpful tool in your astrological toolbox to see what's coming up. I have given several presentations about these charts to show how useful they are and how to set them up. There are always so many wonderful questions at the end of each session, which can bring up some excellent points. I'll close with a few more notes from these sessions.

Prediction vs. forecasting

You know, there is a lot that can be done with astrology and one of those things is forecasting. I don't like the word prediction. Prediction makes it seem like you don't have a choice. But with forecasting – you have a choice, it's like you can see down the road a little bit better, easier, clearer. It doesn't sound so dire as prediction, where all my free will has been taken away, or I've been told that something will happen.

Learning to read solunar charts

When I read a solunar chart, the first thing I like to do is ask what natal house is coming to the solunar Ascendant, because that is the house that will take focus for the month. Then as the Moon travels around each house, it's going to highlight that area. One of my students did this every month—and she wasn't even a Virgo. Page after page, aspect after aspect, that's the way she learned to do it.

Inner and outer wheels

I always put the natal chart on the outer wheel and the lunar chart on the inside. I put the natal chart on the outside of the wheel because otherwise I wouldn't have a house system to know what's being pulled up, or know what house to focus on. If I used my natal chart in the center, then every month I would have the same house being aspected because the Sun would always come to the same place.

Personal new Moon

I always put the new Moon and the full Moon in charts. When the Moon is opposite your natal Moon, that is called your *personal full Moon*. Things usually come to light around your personal full Moon—which naturally is about two weeks after the new Moon. Go to the ephemeris to see on what date the transiting Moon enters the house you are interested in, enter it on your chart in the proper house, and follow it around.

Distance between the Sun and Moon

I've often wondered about the distance between the Sun and Moon. For example, my Sun and Moon are 41 degrees apart. Every month, there is going to be a Sun-Moon at 41 degrees. It may not be in the same signs as your natal – but it'll still be within that phase of the Moon. That's something worth looking into.

Solunar worksheet notes

RightLeft Graphics has created a worksheet to make it easier to keep track of your solunars. RightLeft Graphics has given permission for owners of this book to photocopy the Solunar Worksheet form for your own use.

A full-size, one-sided worksheet is available from RightLeft Graphics from their website at www.rightleftgraphics.com.

Solunar Worksheet

Name: _____ Date: _____

Birth data: _____

1. Progressed ☉: _____ Angles: _____

2. Progressed ☽: _____ Date: _____

   _____   _____

   _____   _____

3. Solar Arc: _____

4. New and Full ☽ and Eclipses for 2010 (PST/PDT) (se)=solar eclipse, (le)=lunar eclipse

New ☽	Full ☽	Notes/Midpoint trees
Jan. 14 (se) . . 25° ♑ 01'	Jan. 29 . . . . 10° ♌ 15'	
Feb. 13 . . . . . 25° ♒ 18'	Feb. 28 . . . . 9° ♍ 59'	
Mar. 15 . . . . . 25° ♓ 10'	Mar. 29 . . . . . . .9° ♎ 17'	
Apr. 14 . . . . . 24° ♈ 27'	Apr. 28 . . . . 8° ♏ 07'	
May 13 . . . . . 23° ♉ 09'	May 27 . . . . 6° ♐ 33'	
Jun. 12 . . . . . . 21° ♊ 24'	Jun. 26 (le) . . . . . 4° ♑ 46'	
Jul. 11 (se) . . 19° ♋ 24'	Jul. 25 . . . . 3° ♒ 00'	
Aug. 9 . . . . . . 17° ♌ 25'	Aug. 24 . . . . .1° ♓ 26'	
Sep. 8 . . . . . . 15° ♍ 41'	Sep. 23 . . . . 0° ♈ 15'	
Oct. 7 . . . . . . 14° ♎ 24'	Oct. 22 . . . . . . .29° ♈ 33'	
Nov. 5 . . . . . . 13° ♏ 40'	Nov. 21 . . . . 29° ♉ 18'	
Dec. 5 . . . . . . 13° ♐ 28'	Dec. 21 (le) . . . . 29° ♊ 21'	

5. Solunar to Natal Chart: _____

   _____

   _____

6. Midpoints in Natal Chart: ☽/☉ _____ Asc/MC _____

   _____

7. Midpoints in Solunar Chart: ☽/☉ _____ Asc/MC _____

_____

8. Prenatal Solar Eclipse: _____ Prenatal Lunar Eclipse: _____ Other: _____

Arabic Parts: _____

9.

	Natal	Antiscia	^{N}Decl.	Long equiv.	Draconic
☉					
☽					
☿					
♀					
♂					
♃					
♄					
♅					
♆					
♀					
☊					
Asc					
MC					
Vx					

10. Misc info: Relocated A _____ M _____ OOB _____

_____

11. Notes: _____

_____

_____